Ir

Gwen,

Thanks for the support. Hope you enjoy!

Outskirts Press, Inc.
Denver, Colorado

This is a work of fiction. The events and characters described herein are imaginary and are not intended to refer to specific places or living persons. The opinions expressed in this manuscript are solely the opinions of the author and do not represent the opinions or thoughts of the publisher.

Outskirts Press, Inc.
http://www.outskirtspress.com

ISBN: 978-1-4327-1890-9

PRINTED IN THE UNITED STATES OF AMERICA

Acknowledgements

First, I would like to start off by thanking Jehovah and Jesus Christ for giving me the ability and creativity to write, the several patents I hold, as well as the many other talents I possess.

I want to give a huge thank you to my mother *Rosa Lee Bolden* and deceased father *Ira Lee Sherrod* for having me. Because of the life they gave me, I have accomplished many great things at a young age and have a whole lot more in store.

To my sisters: *Brandi and Tanishia Bolden*, brother *Raymond Bolden*, best friend *Jenifer Trautman*, family, and friends. Thank you for the love and support over the years. I can truly say that I am blessed to have the people who surround me.

I didn't want to start naming particular people because it would be just like writing another book but I have to give a special thanks to Dzynhaus.com, the future of design, who masterminded the cover of this book and all my patents. *Tony, Rob, Andre, and Miguel,* thank you for always exceeding my expectations.

I thank you all so much. Love you.

Buckle your seat belts and put your shades on! This shooting star is about to take off!

Introduction

It was the mid seventies. Around those times were the days that hippies existed. Hippies were known for excessive partying, drug, and alcohol abuse. My mother didn't work because my father would not allow her to. She kept the house in order and took me to and from school. My father on the other hand was the provider of the family. He did not spend much time at home. He was always on the go, but we did not lack for anything. I used to ask my father what type of work he was involved in, and he would always respond by saying he was a salesman. The type of business he was involved in was a risky one. One day, I finally realized the type of salesman he really was.

Chapter 1

Samantha

On a usual Friday night in Brooklyn, my friends and I were playing in the park directly across the street from my apartment building. I noticed there was a lot of movement coming from our apartment window. I ran upstairs and witnessed something that would change my life forever. When I entered the door, I saw three men in ski masks. Two of them had on blue masks and the other wore a black one. One of the men in the blue and the one in the black mask restrained my father. The other man in the blue mask had my mother tied to a chair. When I entered the room, the ski mask man in the black pointed a gun at me. He told me to lock the door and take the seat next to my mother. It was obvious; the ski mask man in black was the leader because he did all the talking. With a tight arm grip around my father's neck, he furiously said, "*It didn't have to come to this. I gave you several opportunities to come up with half of my money and you couldn't do that. This reminds me of the last time I had to kill someone, but it was a little different. Not only did he owe me money, but I also caught him cheating with my wife. I killed his kids in front of the two of them before I took care of him and my wife. I hate to say it, but I kind of miss my brother.*"

"*Come on man. You don't have to do this. I'll have the money in two weeks. Please don't do this in front of my family. They don't have anything to do with this. Let them go. You already have me,*" pleaded my father.

With a strong slap of the gun, the gunman replied, "*Shut the hell up! You had a chance to fix this problem and you failed. Now I'm going to get rid of the problem, but before I kill you there is something I want you to see.*"

The man holding my mother down told her to be still and if she screamed, he would shoot her. In a crying voice, my mother begged, "*Please don't! Not in front of my daughter. I'm begging you. Please!*"

Very aggressively, the gunman tore my mothers clothes off and had his way with her in front of my father and I. I couldn't bare to watch it, so I closed my eyes and cried my heart away. They made my father watch his wife get raped right in front of his eyes. For the first time, my father felt helpless. He couldn't do anything but cry. As soon as the gunmen finished with my mother, I heard three gunshots. Immediately, the gunmen left without leaving a shred of evidence or chance of being caught. With my eyes remaining shut for the fear of seeing my father shot, I sat there shaking to as if I had seen a ghost. My mother stood over my father crying while watching him gasp for breath. On his very last breath, my father shed a tear, looking my mother in the eyes and said, *"I love you."*

One week from the day of his death, my father was buried in his hometown, Brownsville about an hour south of where we were living. The reality of seeing him in a casket was very painful. This was the first time I had been to a funeral and it scared me greatly. Just as he wished, his casket was pearl white and his suit was jet black. Even though this was a very sad moment, I have to say the mortuary prepared his body well for the funeral service.

The first couple of months were very hard. My mother and I moved down to New Jersey to live with my grandmother. The living conditions were much different. My grandmother lived in a four-bedroom house. There were three families living there: My uncle Tony, his wife and their two kids and my aunt Stacy with her four children. Then, there was my mother and I.

My grandmother's name is Ella Mae Green. She was originally from Georgia. Her parents were children of slavery. At the tender age of 15 years old, she ran away to New Jersey to be with my grandfather, Charles Green. I never had the honor of meeting him, but heard many great stories about him. He died before I was born. He was ten years older than my grandmother was. The laws weren't strict, then. Older men taking young girls to marry and have children, was common in those days. My grandmother had five children in all. Two of which died at birth.

Aunt Stacy was the oldest child. She had what people would call, the *"Baby Daddy Syndrome."* Her children were from three different men. Only one of them helped take care is his child. He was a father, not a daddy. The other two were straight *"Deadbeats."* Aunt Stacy was a great mother. She would give her last to make sure her children lacked for nothing. Her job as a cashier didn't pay much, but she always found a way to make something out of nothing.

Uncle Tony was the leech of the family. He would take advantage of anything or anyone if allowed to. Uncle Tony was the second oldest child, but acted like the baby. Since he was the only boy, my grandmother treated him like one. He couldn't keep a job any longer than two weeks. His complaints were that the jobs didn't pay enough, like he had some special training or something. They say a man doesn't know himself until he knows the type of woman he chooses. In Uncle Tony's case, this statement is true because his wife was the same way.

The first week at my grandma's house had to be a collection of the longest nights of my life. When my father was alive, he provided everything I needed and almost everything I wanted. My mother never worked during the 17 years she and my father were together. Now that my father was no longer around she had to find work and help out with the bills around the house. After a few weeks of job searching she found part time work at a local diner as a waitress. The income was not great, but it helped out a lot. As the rock of the family, my grandmother was the one everyone depended on. During her journey through life, she gained much experience and seemed to have the answer to everything. Sitting on the front porch, my grandma waited for my mother to arrive home to talk to her. When my mother walked up the steps, my grandmother sat her down.

"*I been sitting here waiting on you. It's been a spell since we had a mother to daughter talk. You know they have always said a mother knows her children better than they know themselves. Whether good or bad, we know what is going on. So, tell me what is bothering you, my child,*" asked my grandmother.

"*I just don't know where to start. I'm so used to William being around and providing for our family. I feel lost without him. He was the foundation of our house-*

hold. I know the way he lived his life was not right, but he was a true father, friend, and husband. It's so hard to let go after almost 18 years of being with him," wept my mother.

"*I understand where you are coming from but you have to move on. When your father died, I felt the same way. I never completely relied on him because you cannot put all your trust in man. Trust in God and He will never lead you astray. Pray, pray and pray! He is the only one that can get you through any situation. You have a whole new life to begin now. Be strong for Samantha. She needs you now more than she ever did before. It's a rough time for you both. You have to be there for each other. I love you baby.*"

"*I love you too.*"

Because of the neighborhood in which my grandmother lived, I had to attend a predominately white school. At first, I hated it because I was not use to being around white kids. I missed my friends back home. Not having my father around really took a toll on my life. I had no desire to attend school, play, or make any new friends. My grades began to decline. My grandmother thought it would be best if I started seeing a therapist. Twice a week, I would have an hour-long session.

After three weeks on the job, my mom became sick. The illness lasted for more than two weeks. Finally, she decided to visit a doctor for a checkup. To her surprise, mom found out that she was three months pregnant. The last person my mother had been with was the gunman who raped her. He did not have on any protection and she wasn't on any birth control. She knew it wasn't my father's because he couldn't have any more children due to an accident he had shortly after I was born. She and my father made several attempts to have another child, but were unsuccessful. Nothing in the world could have prepared her for this shocking news. On the way home, she pondered the best way to inform the family. As she stumbled through the door, with tears pouring down her face, my grandmother rushed towards her with open arms.

"*What's wrong? Is everything ok? Take a deep breath, relax and let it go,*" suggested my grandmother.

"*I'm pregnant,*" my mother cried out.

"*I thought something was really wrong. That's nothing to be sad about, baby. You should be happy. You and William had been trying so hard after Samantha.*"

"*You don't understand. There is something I didn't tell you. William couldn't have any more kids because of an accident he had after Samantha was born. Before he was murdered, one of the men raped me in front of him and Samantha. I wanted to fight back, scream or just do something, but I was afraid they would have harmed her. I felt like I let them both down because I felt so helpless and afraid. A mother is supposed to protect her children in times of danger. I couldn't do anything."*

"*You're right. You couldn't do anything. If you could have, you would have. You did what any normal person would do. Only a fool would have tried to stop a man with a gun in his face.*"

"*I didn't want to say anything because I was too embarrassed to tell anyone.*"

"*Baby, you have nothing to be ashamed of. Many people have gone through similar events. I know you feel violated in the worst way, but once you get pass this trial it will only make you stronger. Time will heal those wounds.*"

"*What should I do about the baby?*"

"*What do you mean?*"

"*I don't want to be pregnant.*"

"*Don't you dare think about that. I know your heart is speaking with anger right now but you have to do what's right in the eyes of God. Taking an innocent life is not the answer. You would be just as guilty as the man who did this to you. We'll get through this together.*"

"*How should I tell Samantha?*"

"*Leave that up to me. You're dealing with enough. I can get through to her better right now.*"

After my grandmother broke the news to me about my mother's pregnancy, I was a little jealous at first. I was used to being the only child. Now that my father was no longer there, everything was much harder on us. This may sound selfish, but we were already struggling and now we had to struggle more because of a baby that didn't come from my father. My mother and I never had a good mother and daughter relationship. It's probably because of the fact that I was a daddy's girl. Now that she was depressed and expecting, she acted as if I didn't exist.

After attending therapy sessions for a few weeks, I was starting to become myself again. I started making friends and having fun. My teacher noticed my willingness to participate in class activities. The first friend I made was a little white girl named Erica. I asked her where she got her name from because it sounded like a black girl's name. If you did not know her, you would have sworn she was black. She claimed her style came from watching videos. Erica lived with her father, Thomas, and stepmother, Mary Ann. Her mother passed shortly after she was born. She was killed in a car accident caused by a drunk driver. Mary Ann had been in Erica's life since she was 1 year old. They were very close and Erica called her mom. Her father, on the other hand, reminded me of my father. He was the breadwinner of the family, but was never home. Tom was an investment banker that traveled much of the year doing business. Their house was crazy! It was a three-story mansion located in an upscale neighborhood. I'm talking about some Princess Diana stuff. The house was so big; they had a maid, cook, and driver to chauffeur Erica to and from school. I had never seen anything like this in the projects. My mother wasn't a great cook or driver. Every weekend, I asked to sleep over Erica's so I could have a taste of the good life. Dolls were not on my radar anymore. I was trying to figure out how I could get me a house like theirs when I got older. Whenever Mr. Tom was home I would ask him a lot of questions about the business. Seeing my interest, Mr. Tom took me to work with him several times on "Bring Your Child To Work" Day. It was a fast paced atmosphere and I loved it. He would have me complete few assignments for him as if I was his assistant. I was excited to work with him. Mr. Tom made me feel as though I had a father again.

Three months had passed since my mother found out about her pregnancy. Time had healed her wounds a little. On this day she was scheduled for a sonogram. I was kind of anxious to know what she would be having, despite the circumstance. A little brother would be cool to have because I did not care for dolls anymore. The doctor walked in the room smiling and spoke.

"*Good afternoon, Mrs. Bennett. How are you feeling?*"

In a nonchalant tone she answered, "*Fine. I guess.*"

"*Ok. I need you to lay back and relax. Take a deep breath and hold. Now let go. Good. Take one more and release. Great! Now we are going to do the sonogram. Excited to find out what you are having?*"

"*A little.*"

"*Which one do you prefer? Having a boy or girl?*"

"*It doesn't matter much.*"

The doctor dimmed the lights so that the sonogram could be seen clearer. He started rubbing this jelly-looking stuff on her stomach. He then moved the wand around to locate the baby's position.

"*I see something here, but it is hard to make out. I need for you to turn on your side. See here. There is the head, legs and arms. Let's see this from another angle.*"

The sound that was coming from her stomach sounded like a seashell when you put your ear next to it. Once he found the heartbeat, it sounded irregular. The doctor knew something was not right. It could have been one of two problems. Either the baby's heart was working too hard or there were two of them in her stomach.

With excitement, the doctor told my mother, "*You are not going to believe this. There are two of them.*"

Not so excited, my mother replied, "*Oh my God! What are they?*"

"*The first one is a girl. Turn to the other side. I'm going to press on your stomach to try and make the baby move. It won't hurt. You'll just feel a little pressure. There it is. It's another girl. Two girls. Congratulations!*"

Mom was in shock. The only words that came out were, "*Are we done yet?*"

The results of my mother's sonogram were far too overwhelming for her. Not only was she struggling to take care of she and I, now she had to support two unexpected babies.

Falling close to her seventh month of pregnancy, she was forced to quit her job due to sickness. Since she was expecting twins, her pregnancy was predicted to last no longer than eight months. If it were not for my grandmother's social security check and the little bit of money she set aside for so many years, things would have been much harder. We did not have much, but we did what we had to do in order to survive. Mr. Tom knew of our situation, so he let me work with him to earn a few dollars to help the family. It was cool because I gained experience in what it felt like to earn an income. An investment banker was definitely what I wanted to be when I grew up.

Just as fast as things were getting better, they started to take a turn for the worst. Only three months after finding out that she was having twins, my mother was admitted into the hospital for high blood pressure. Her stress was causing the babies to become stressed. The doctors had no choice but to do an emergency c-section. After almost eight months of pregnancy, my mother gave birth to the twin girls. The first one was named Riana; she was 12 inches long and weighed 4 lbs 3oz. The second girl was named Briana. She too, was 12 inches long but weighed 5 lbs.

even. My mother didn't get to see the babies at first. For some reason, she passed out during the surgery. I must admit they were two of the prettiest babies I had ever seen. Within a blink of an eye, my jealousy went away and love settled in. I started to plan all the fun things that we were going to do with each other. When my mother awoke, she was greeted by all of our family members with flowers, balloons, and gifts.

Together the family said, "*Congratulations*!"

"*Hey baby! How are you feeling?*" asked my grandmother while rubbing my mother's head to soothe her.

"A little weak. I need something to drink", answered my mother.

Being crazy as usual, my Uncle Tony said, *"Those babies look just like you and William except they're not ugly. Just joking! They are beautiful like you lil sis."*

"Congratulations sis!" said Aunt Stacy. *"They are adorable! You should be thankful for your two blessings. I know William would be so proud."*

"I am. Where are they?" replied my mother.

"The nurse took them away to clean them up and check their vitals", stated Aunt Stacy.

"Can I see them?" asked my mother.

"Let me check. I'll go and ask one of the nurses", said Aunt Stacy as she walked toward the door.

Before Aunt Stacy could make it through the door, my

mother let out this big sigh of pain.

"Ouch", shouted my mother.

"What's wrong?" asked my grandmother.

As she began to talk, a clot of blood could be seen in her mouth.

"I don't know but my stomach is killing me. Please get the doctor!"

"Don't move. Try to stay still. Stacy, hurry! Go and get the doctor."

Aunt Stacy hurried out the door yelling in broken English, *"Ay! Ay! Where da nurses at?"*

Quickly uplifting herself from the chair, Nurse Shelly asked, *"What's wrong?"*

"My sister just coughed up blood. She says her stomach is hurting", answered Aunt Stacy.

As the nurse rushed into the room, you could tell from the expression on her face that she already knew what was going on.

"What type of pain is it?"

"My lower stomach is killing me", my mother replied.

"Ok. Let me get a hold of the doctor."

The nurse immediately left the room and paged the doctor. When Dr. Bernstein heard the page, he immediately returned the call. *"This is Dr. Bernstein."*

"The patient in room 283B is complaining of lower abdominal pains and is also regurgitating blood. What should we do?"

"Let's hurry her back up to surgery. We need to scan her to see if the bleeding has stopped."

After hanging up the phone with the doctor, the nurse came back into the room to explain to the family what needed to be done.

"Ma'am, we have to get you back upstairs to run more tests."

"What's the problem?" asked my grandmother.

"Well ma'am, during the cesarean, the doctor who did the cutting went too deep and probably caused some damage."

"How is that possible? What type of doctors do ya'll have working here? If he doesn't know what he's doing, he shouldn't be cutting on anybody."

"Ma'am I understand how you feel but I don't have time to answer questions at this moment. We need to get her upstairs ASAP."

After running the tests, Dr. Bernstein knew exactly what the problem was. He had to go back in to try and stop the bleeding from the cut during the cesarean. After several hours of attempting to stop the bleeding and watching my mother's heart rate decline, the doctors knew there wasn't much more they could do for her. They tried several attempts to revive her but were not successful.

I remember like it was yesterday when the doctor, covered with blood, came into the room with this devastated look on his face and said, "I'm sorry, but we couldn't save her. The bleeding was too severe. We tried our best to stop it, but there was nothing we could do.

At the top of her lungs, my grandmother yelled, *"No! No! No! Lord Jesus, Why?"*

On May 26, 1978 at 8:37 pm, my mother was pronounced dead, only eight months after my father. I didn't know whether I wanted to cry or faint. Imagine an eight years old losing both of their parents in the same year. Devastating is an understatement. I'm going to tell you something. No pain is greater than losing your parents. Love them like everyday is the last day you will be able to see, touch or tell them how much you love them. Death is like a thief in the night. You know it is out there, but you don't know when it will strike.

Now that my mother has passed, someone had to take custody of my twin sisters and I. The only person I felt comfortable with was my grandmother. After discussing our situation with the nurses, Aunt Stacy had to inform my grandmother about the situation that was at hand.

"Momma. I know this isn't the best time but we need to know who is going to take in the twins. I mean..."

"My heart is broken right now. I can't make a decision about that right now. Besides baby, I'm tired. I don't know how much longer I can make it. I'm not getting any younger. My days of raising children are far-gone. My

baby just passed at the age of 41 years old. I love my grandchildren with all my heart, but this is too much for me to handle on my own."

"I'm sorry. You're right. There's just so much happening at once."

"It's fine. I love you!"

"Love you too, ma!"

Since no one in our immediate family was stable enough to take in my sisters, they had to be put up for adoption. My grandmother and I were allowed visitation rights until both girls found families. I had a blast playing with my sisters. The time went by so fast. Four weeks after their birth, the social worker Deborah Anderson found both of the twins' families. Since the Department of Children and Family Services could not find a family that would take in both of the twins, they had to be separated and placed with two different families. Riana went to a newly married African American couple that couldn't bare children on their own, so their only other option was to adopt. Their names were Frank and Stephanie Johnson. Frank was a 32-year-old construction foreman who made a good salary for a guy his age. He grew up in a single parent household with his two older sisters. His father was never around, so the streets raised him. At the age of 16, he was sentenced to three years in jail for drugs and weapon charges. During his time served, he realized that his life was headed for destruction, so he made a change and turned away from the gang life. The only way to be totally free from gang involvement was through death. Once you joined, there was no getting out. Since Frank was well respected on the streets, nothing ever happened to him. Stephanie was a 29-year-old assistant who worked for a private medical practice. She and her two brothers were raised by both of their parents. After she graduated from high school, her parents separated. Their love for each other faded away years before they separated. They stayed together for the their children's sake. She remembered all the good times she had while growing up with her family, and this is why she was so eager to start her own. Frank and Stephanie met four years prior to adopting. After three and a half years of dating, Frank finally decided to marry Stephanie because of her threats to leave him. Similar to my father, he couldn't have children due to an accident he had on the job. It didn't bother him much because he was in no rush to have children, unlike Stephanie. Thirty was knocking at the door for her and she didn't want to wait too late to raise children. Recently, they purchased a home just west of town. The area they lived in was not too far from gang territory. It was not in the area of their choice, but their income would not allow them to move to a suburban neighborhood.

Briana was adopted by a white American lesbian couple named Danielle and Susan Lovinski. Of course, they could not have children together. Instead of one of them being artificially inseminated, they decided to take the adoption route. Despite the way they lived their lives; they both were great people. They both came from well-grounded families where unity was the most important key to happiness. Knowing there were babies in children services for disturbing reasons bothered them. The only way they could help make a difference in one of the children's lives was to adopt them and show them the love they should receive. Danielle was a 30-year-old attorney who graduated from the Harvard School of Law. She owned her own firm with two other partners. Her father was a judge and her mother was an attorney. It was obvious that she would follow in the footsteps of her parents. Her relationship with her father was not as good as she hoped due to the lifestyle she lived. On the other hand, her mother was more acceptable of the situation but did not approve of it either. Susan was a 31-year-old successful real estate broker. Her father was a neurosurgeon and her mother was a geologist. After thirty years of marriage, her mother left her father because she could not live a double life anymore. Her mother was also a lesbian and had been for all thirty years of marriage. Susan didn't grow up seeing her mother as a lesbian, but adapted to the lifestyle very fast. She and Danielle met at a nightclub three years ago and had been dating since then. They were the best of friends as well as mates. The two did not argue or disagree much. They took their relationship to the next level by getting married and planning to have a child. It was the reason why they decided to adopt.

It was a Wednesday afternoon when the Johnson's came to pick up Riana. This was the first time they had seen my sister and it would be my last.

"Good evening Mr. And Mrs. Johnson. Today is your big day! Are you excited?" asked Deborah.

"Very excited, but a little nervous at the same time. I could not sleep last night because I was so anxious for this moment to come," replied Stephanie with a huge smile on her face.

"It's perfectly fine to be nervous. After all this is a huge responsibility you're taking on. Most people have the wrong perception about raising children. They think when the child turns eighteen their job is finished, but parenting lasts a lifetime. Don't worry. You will be fine. What about you, Frank? Are you equally excited as well or are you the conservative type?"

With a nonchalant attitude, he answered, *"Oh yeah. Sure."*

"Wait right here and I'll go get her."

As soon as Deborah left the room Stephanie got upset with Frank and confronted him.

"That was so phony. You could at least fake like you're happy. Anyone could have seen through that fake smile."

"Whatever! What do you want me to do? Jump around

and dance?"

"I'm not saying you had to do all that, but..."

In the midst of their argument, Deborah walked back in the room with the baby and said, *"Here she is. She is so adorable, isn't she?"*

Overly excited, Stephanie replied, *"Oh my God! Yes, she is beautiful!"*

"Riana, say hello to your new mommy."

"Look at those chubby cheeks. They make you want to bite them. Thank you very much Ms. Anderson!"

"No, thank you! This is a great thing you are doing. It takes a warm-hearted person to take in a child that doesn't belong to you. God has favor in his eyes for you. You are blessed to have this blessing. There is one more thing before you go. Riana has an older sister out front. If you don't mind, I would like for her to see Riana one last time."

Stephanie was so emotional that she started crying tears of joy.

"No problem."

At this point in my life, if I had known anything about suicide I probably would have attempted it. First, my father had passed. Then, my mother passed. Now, my sisters have been taken away. All this in one year was too much for anyone. I was happy for them because they had a home to go to and someone to care for them. On the other hand, I'm sad to not have them to grow with.

Deborah brought Riana to my grandmother and I so we could say our goodbyes.

"Ms. Green. I know this is a rough time for you, but I thought you would like to see your granddaughter one more time before she leaves," said Deborah as she handed Riana to her.

"I thank you very much! It was very thoughtful of you", my grandma stated.

Riana was too young to understand what grandma was saying to her but the look in her eyes seemed as if she could. With a tear in her eye, my grandmother kissed her on the cheek and said, *"Well, I guess this is it, little one. You take care you hear? Your mother would have been so proud. I won't be around in flesh, but my spirit will always be with you. I love you so much!"*

She then reached towards me and passed me the baby.

"Here. Give your sister a hug and tell her you love her."

I was so nervous that my hands were sweating and my legs were shaking. In a sad and very hurtful voice, I said, *"Bye. I love you."*

After I gave her a kiss, Ms. Deborah took her away and that was the last time I would see her. My grandmother knew I was very sad when I started crying. She told me, *"Don't cry baby. I know you're hurt. We all are. Everything is going to be ok. One day, you will be able to see her again. Sometimes life throws challenges at us that we can't control or handle. This situation is one of those challenging times. You still have me to love you. What can I do to make you happy?"*

"I don't know."

"How about some ice cream? Does that sound good?"

"Yes ma'am."

"Grab your coat. It's raining outside."

As my grandmother drove away, I stared out the rainy back window watching my sister being carried away by her new foster parents and watched a part of my life disappear.

Chapter 2

The Departing

It's been almost thirteen years since my parents passed and still I haven't got used to the fact that they are gone. Some nights, I wake up in cold sweats when I dream about my father's death. Still, to date, I go to therapy for that reason.

"So tell me Samantha, how are you feeling?" asked Dr. Whittaker.

"Everyday is different. Some days are good and others are hard to deal with. It's been almost thirteen years, but still I hear those gunshots and that gunman's disturbing voice."

"I can not say how you feel because I wasn't there and have not been through a situation like this before, but you

have to try and get past this or it will haunt you for the rest of your life. Sometimes bad things happen to us beyond our control. In time we have to heal those wounds and move on with our lives. Do you get out much?"

"Not really. My friends always ask me to go out but I'm always so busy with school and work. By the time the weekend gets here, I'm exhausted. Besides, I go and see my grandmother on the weekends."

"Let's make a deal. This weekend, I want you to go out with your girlfriends and have a good time. Go dancing, skating, or whatever. Just relax, be free, and mingle. If that doesn't work, the next session is free of charge. Do you think you can handle the challenge?"

"I think I can."

"Well I guess that's it. Remember to relax and have fun! That's the key."

"Thanks a lot, Doc. I needed that."

"No problem. That's what I am here for."

As soon as I left Dr. Whittaker's office, Erica called my phone.

"Greetings!"

"Hey girl. What you doing?"

"Oh, nothing. Just leaving the therapist's office."

"Girl, you still doing that? I don't know why you keep wasting your money. I told you what you need to do."

"And exactly, what would that be?"

"You need to go out and have fun. Then, you will get your mind off that."

"That's the same thing Dr. Whittaker told me."

"Most importantly, you need one of those young, dark and sexy brothers to come and blow your back out."

"I don't need my back blown out, as you so eloquently put it. It has been a long time, but getting laid won't solve my problems."

"I don't know about you, but I had a few problems of my own. Now... whoo, they gone, honey."

"You so crazy!"

"And you know it! So are we going out or what?"

"I guess. I don't know where to go."

"Leave that part up to me. I gots the hookup. Be ready around nine."

"Will do."

"Love you!"

"Love you too, crazy girl. Bye."

During our senior year in high school, Erica and I decided to go off to college together. She was my best friend and I enjoyed being around her. To earn some extra cash, Mr. Thomas allowed me work for him from home. It was considered an internship, since my degree was in finance. As soon as I graduate he has a position reserved for me in his firm. The starting salary is not what I expected, but I could live with it. Besides, his office was a pleasant environment to work in and that's an important attribute when working for a company.

Later on that night, while preparing to go out, Erica called me to make sure I was still going. She thought I would back out.

"What heffa? Yes, I'm still going."

"Why do I have to be all that? And how do you know I was calling about that?"

"Because I know you."

"Well, you're right. I know you too and I know you will change your mind in a heartbeat. Are you getting ready?"

"Yes, mother. I am."

"Good. What are you wearing?"

"This little skirt and halter-top I bought today and some heels. Why? You are not borrowing anymore of my shoes until you return the other four pair."

"I was not going to ask you that, but since you mentioned it. What kind of black shoes do you have over there?"

I hate the fact that Erica and I wear the same size clothes and shoes. I might as well start shopping for *our* clothes instead of *my* clothes, because she wears them more than I do.

"Come get what you need and bring my other stuff back."

"Thanks, honey. Love ya!"

"Whatever!"

As soon as I got off the phone with Erica, my phone rang again. I answered the phone annoyed.

"Hello."

"Hey Beanie. What's wrong with you?" asked Aunt Stacy.

Beanie was a name I inherited when I was a little girl. It originated from Aunt Stacy because I was so skinny and then the rest of the family started calling me by that name too. They said that I reminded them of a string bean, straight up and down. The name used to bother me because my cousins would tease me a lot, but not anymore. I filled out just right.

"I'm trying to get ready to go out and my phone keeps ringing."

"Besides that, is everything else ok?"

"Yes. I'm fine, but it sounds like something is bothering you."

By the tone of her voice, I knew something was wrong. All day, I had a funny feeling that something was not right. I just couldn't put my finger on it.

"Well, it's momma. She's not doing well right now. She didn't want to go to the hospital so we called in a nurse and it doesn't sound good."

"What did she say?"

"She said her health is rapidly declining and her memory is going. She may have a month, week or even days to live. Who knows? The nurse is going to come back in a few days if she is not doing better."

"I pray that she is going to be fine."

"We all are, but the fact is she is getting older and one day we knew we would have to face these times. Don't worry yourself. We all have to face this path in life. Whether you accept it or not, it has to happen. The only thing we can do is try to get closer to God and hope that He accepts us in His new kingdom. Life is short. Live it the right way and do good by others and the rest is easy. So you go ahead and finish getting ready. Don't let this spoil your fun. Have a great time. Grandma will be fine".

"I will. I love you."

"I will call you if anything changes. Take care and I love you too."

At that moment, I really did feel like backing out on Erica, but I made a promise to her and Dr. Whittaker. My grandmother is the only parent I have left in my life. I once heard that an adult doesn't become a real man or woman until they lose their parents. It made sense because no matter how old you are, if your parents are still alive you can call on them in times of need. When they are gone, you have no one to lean on. This is when you have to step up to the plate and make things happen for yourself.

I was not going to let the bad news spoil my night. It's been a long time since I've had any fun. I'm going to have some drinks and whatever happens after that, happens. As expected, Erica arrived to my place late.

"Girl! I was about to change my mind. A few minutes more and you would have been going by yourself."

"Don't act like that. You know I got some sister in me."

"And what is that supposed to mean?"

"I'm late for everything, just like ya'll."

"Anyways! Don't go there with me."

"It's a joke. What's your problem?"

"My Aunt Stacy just called and said my grandmother is not doing well."

"What did she say the problem was?"

"She has been diabetic for years and now she is in her final stages. The nurse doesn't expect her to make it much longer."

"I'm so sorry! Do you still want to go out?"

"Yes. Staying in this house won't make me feel any better. Besides, you were right. I do need a drink and somebody to come solve some of my problems."

"I know that's right. Where are the shoes?"

"Your rentals are way over due. Where are my other shoes?"

"I was rushing to get over here and forgot."

"Don't make me hurt you. Let's go."

On our way out, I still didn't know where we were going. But knowing Erica, it was probably somewhere so ghetto that I wouldn't go there and I'm the one who is black.

"Where are we going?"

"Rasheed told me about this new spot across town."

"Rasheed? The Rasheed? Girl, you're still wasting your time on him? I know if he recommended a place, it must not be good. Where is the dance floor? In his bedroom? That's the only place he wants to move his body."

"Girl, relax. I think you will like this place. Besides, a few other people recommended it to me also. I can't stand your booshy behind. I'm the white girl and I'm more down to earth than you."

"It better be. You know I don't like ghetto events. I would walk out of there as fast as I walked in. For the record, I'm not booshy baby, it's called classy."

I must admit, from the look of the outside of the club, I was wrong. It was very nice and looked new. The bouncers wore suits, the lines had velvet ropes and the dress code was strictly enforced. The lines were very long, so we went in V.I.P. I liked V.I.P because most of the immature, broke guys wouldn't pay the price to go in the area. There were mostly high-class men in here. Some were fake, but it was easy to spot them out.

On this night, the club was live. There were a lot of cute guys in there, but only one of them really caught my attention.

"Girl, do you see that one over there?"

"Yes! Yes! Yes! He is so fine. He keeps looking over here at you. Go talk to him."

"Hell no! I don't step to guys. That's not my style. If he wants to talk to me he will come over here."

"You are so stuck up; it's pathetic. I'm going to let him know you want to talk to him."

"Don't play with me. If he wants to talk to me, he will come over here."

As soon as I turned my back Erica must have gave him a hand signal to get his attention because he came right over.

"Bye girl. I'll be back. I'm going to find Rasheed."

"Don't..."

"Hey. How are you", he asked with his beautiful smile.

"Um...good."

"I'm Anthony Richmond, but most people call me Jamal."

"Which one do you prefer?"

"It doesn't matter. And you are?"

"Uh...Samantha."

This brother was so fine that he made me nervous. I wanted to skip to the part where I get back problems, but that was not the way I rolled. Well, at least not on the first night.

"Do I make you nervous?"

"Oh no. Not at all."

"Would you like a drink or anything to eat? They have a great menu here".

"I ate before I got here, but I will take something to drink".

God knows I was hungry, but I was acting too shy to eat around him. You know how women are when we act too cute.

"I'm going to let you decide. What do you think I would like?"

"Well, you are a beautiful young lady and seem to be conservative, so I would guess you prefer something light. How does an Amaretto Sour sound?"

This brother was so smooth that it was scary. You could tell he was educated. He dressed nice and smelled good. From the way he talked, it seemed like he had a degree in women.

"Here you are. An Amaretto Sour for you and a bottle of water for me. So, what do you do for a living?"

"I'm in school right now, but I graduate in a few weeks."

"That's great! What is your major?"

"Finance. I have wanted to do this since I was kid."

"That is a strange job to pick as a kid. What was your inspiration?"

"When my mother and I moved down here from New York to live with my grandmother, the living conditions were very different from the way we were use to living. I met my best friend, Erica, and her father, who is an investment banker. Seeing the way they lived made me want to do the same thing as her father. He took me to work with him several times and I fell in love with it. So, here I am. What about you?"

"I graduated two years ago with a degree in accounting. I have not quite put my degree to use because I do much work with my father."

"What does he do?"

"He is a salesman who also does other investments. Actually, this club is one of his investments."

"That's what my father use to tell me until..."

"What?"

"Never mind. I really don't want to discuss that right now."

After talking to Anthony for a couple of hours, I was exhausted and ready to leave. He seemed to be a very sweet and sincere person. I was most impressed by his ability to hold a conversation and keep my attention. I get bored quickly. When you talk to some guys, it's like speaking another language. The negative thing about him was that he obviously has money and he's in the club all the time. So, I know he runs into a lot of women.

Erica must have forgotten about me because I haven't seen her in hours. The club was too crowded for me to walk and find her. I called her on her cell phone. "Where are you?"

"I'm with Rasheed. We left the club for a while. I'll be back in about thirty minutes."

"I'm tired and ready to go. This is the reason why I drive my own car because when I'm ready to go. I leave. You need to hurry up. Bye."

After seeing how angry I was, Anthony offered to take me home.

"I can give you a lift if you're really ready to go. That's if you don't mind riding with a stranger."

In my mind, I wanted to tell him, *"Hell yes,"* and pull him by his arm and drag him out of here.

"Um...I guess that would be fine. I usually do not do this because I don't like for everyone to know where I live. People are so hard to trust."

"I agree. You don't have to worry. I am a trustworthy guy. I'll be on my very best behavior."

"I surely hope so."

When we left the club, he drove me home in his new Mercedes-Benz. I don't know if he drove like this every-day, but it was surely a good look for him. On our way home, we talked more. I learned about some of his dreams and personal goals. This is the first guy I have ever dealt with that has such a high maturity level. I didn't want him to know exactly where I lived, so I had him drop me off a couple of buildings down from my apartment.

"I enjoyed being in your presence tonight. What are the chances of us seeing each other again?"

"Good. I think you are a very sweet person with a great personality. I would like to see you again.

"Thank you. I think you are pretty cool as well. Would you like me to walk you to your door?"

"No. I'll be fine. Give me your number and I will call you."

After giving me his number, he leaned over to kiss me and I stopped him.

"Not too fast. There will be plenty of opportunities later."

I wanted to kiss him but I had a reputation to keep as a young lady. He felt bad and apologized, "Sorry."

"It's fine. No need to be sorry."

"When can I expect a call from you?"

"Soon."

Walking up the stairs to my apartment and trying to store Anthony's number in my phone, I had an incoming call from Erica.

"What heffa?"

"Where are you?"

"I'm walking through my door now."

"You left how long ago and you just getting home? What were you doing?"

"I'm sure no more than what you were doing. We just talked. He wanted to kiss me, but I didn't let him."

"Why?"

"I didn't want to come off as being easy."

"What do you think about him?"

"He was very nice and sweet. I could see myself going out with him."

"Did ya'll exchange numbers?"

"I took his number, but I didn't give him mine."

"When are you going to call him?"

"What's up with all these questions? I will call him in a few days. I don't want to call him right away and seem desperate. What were you doing?"

"You already know. Whoo...my back is hurting."

"I'm going to leave on that note. I have a few things to do tomorrow. Bye."

"Call me. Bye."

When I answered Erica's call I hadn't saved Anthony's number yet, so the phone call deleted the number. I had one drink too many and was too tired to remember what the number was. I could kill Erica right about now. First, she arrived to my house late. Then, she left me at the club and now, she made me lose Anthony's number. I guess this is what friends are for. So to say, I never spoke to him again.

The next morning, I got up and took my normal shower and ate my usual breakfast. There were a lot of preparations that needed to be made before my graduation in a couple of weeks. After I ran all my errands, I decided to go visit my grandmother. She lived about an hour from me. I was tired from the night before and didn't feel like making the drive but her being in the condition she was in, there was no telling what could happen. I didn't want to have any regrets or feel guilty if I were not able to see or talk to her again.

When I arrived at the house, I started feeling nervous. It was probably because I didn't know what to expect. The closer I got to the door, the more I felt like I was going to pass out. When I walked through the door, Aunt Stacy was asleep in the recliner. I softly called her name to wake her, so that I wouldn't scare her out of her sleep.

"Aunt Stacy."

"Hey Beanie. When did you get here?"

"Not even a minute ago. I just walked through the door. Where is grandma?"

"She should be in the room sleeping."

"Is she doing well enough for me to talk to her?"

"Of course. She will be thrilled to see you, but if she's sleeping, try to let her rest. I must warn you though. She has been forgetting a lot of things lately."

When entering the room where my grandmother was sleeping, I tried to open the door slowly so the annoying squeaking sound coming from the hinges wouldn't wake her.

There she was, asleep on the bed, looking helpless. It hurt me so bad to see her in this condition. Especially from a person that's so cheerful and full of life. I started rubbing my hand through her hair and kissed her on the forehead. I didn't know if she would wake up before I left, so I told her how I felt about her anyway.

"Grandma, I know you can hear me. This is Samantha. I love you so much! This is hurting me so bad to see you like this. You've always taught me to love and let go but its so much easier said than done. You have made my life so much easier since my parents passed. I remember when you said that everyone is born into this world and leave as an infant. I didn't know what it meant then, but seeing you in this helpless position makes me understand."

As I was getting ready to leave, she opened her eyes and said, *"Juanita is that you?"*

"No, Grandma. It's me, Samantha."

"Hey baby. How are you?"

"I'm doing ok."

"Where is William?"

Seeing that my grandmother was thinking that I was my mother crushed me more because I wanted to have a heart to heart talk with her. I never imagined seeing her go like this. This gave me insight on how sick she really was.

"He's not here. How are you feeling?"

"Well, this old body of mine is tired. I don't know how much longer I can hold on. Life comes at you so fast. If you don't prepare yourself for the unexpected, it will take you down. I must admit. My life has been a rollercoaster. I've seen some good days and Lord knows I've had my share of bad ones, but by the grace of God I held on strong. I know family isn't what it use to be, but next to God, it's all we have. He is the creator and can't nobody deliver out of any problem the way that He can. Remember, He is a jealous God. He doesn't want you to put anybody before him. Walk righteous and the rest is easy."

"I don't want you to go. You are the only one I have left."

"I can't be here with you forever. Now is the time for you to become a woman. I want you to make me a promise that you will never give up. When times are hard, you have to keep pushing and when you feel like you can't push no more, dig deep and find that inner strength to keep moving. Nobody is gonna do anything for you. If you want it, you have to do it for yourself. Even when I'm not here, I will still always be with you. If you look around for someone and no one is there, look inside your heart and I'll be there with you. Everything is going to be fine."

Before she could finish talking, her eyes were slowly

shutting again. I didn't want to wake her because I knew how vital her resting was. I kissed her on the head again and left because I still had to study for finals. When I walked out of the room, Aunt Stacy was still sitting in the recliner. She could tell by the redness of my eyes that I had been crying.

"Are you ok?" she asked.

"Not really, but I'll be fine."

"I understand. It's very hard to see her go from the way she was to this point. Did you get a chance to talk to her?"

"Yes and No. She thought I was my mother and then started asking about my father. After I told her it was me, she started getting deep into one of her life lessons. I think she was really trying to tell me something, but she couldn't stay awake."

"I know. I cried when she thought I was her sister. They say before you lose your memory, flashbacks start to recirculate through your head. The feeling is unexplainable for your mother to not recognize who you are. Do not stress yourself too much. Just remember what she taught us. Love and let go. Take care and drive safely. Let me know when you make it home. Love you!"

"I will. Love you, too!"

My mind was so distorted that I started driving the wrong way home. I didn't realize it until I was ten miles down the highway. Something inside of me was telling me that she knew she would be gone very soon. My grandmother was the only parent I had left. I spent more years with her than I did with my parents. The thought of me becoming a woman was not so tough because I am a very independent person. It was more about not having her around to share all the special moments in life with.

When I got home, I took a shower and put on my nightclothes. I knew I would eventually fall asleep while studying for my finals. While studying, Erica kept calling my phone so I turned it off. Despite the fact that I was studying, I really was not in the mood to talk. After about two hours of studying, I fell asleep. If it weren't for me having to use the bathroom I probably would have slept the whole night through. When I got out of the bathroom I remembered that I had turned my phone off and had forgotten to call Aunt Stacy to let her know that I made it home safely. After I turned my phone on, I saw that I had four voice messages from her. My heart started racing because of the fear of hearing bad news. I hesitated to call her, but knew I had to. I called her back.

"Aunt Stacy. Sorry I missed your calls. I turned my phone off so I could get some studying in and fell asleep."

From the cracking in her voice, I could tell that she had been crying.

"It's okay."

" Is everything ok?"

"Well, grandma..."

Before she could finish talking I dropped the phone and started screaming. I heard Aunt Stacy calling my name to pick up the phone but I couldn't pull myself together. After about thirty minutes of crying I picked up the phone to call her back.

"I'm sorry. I was in too much shock to talk."

"I know. That's why I hung up so you could have your moment. There is no need to be sorry. You have every right to let go of your emotions."

"I knew it. I knew she was trying to tell me her finals words. When did she pass?"

"About three hours after you left. The ambulance came in and took her an hour ago."

"Were you in the room with her?"

"Not at first. I was in the kitchen fixing dinner for everyone and something told me to go in the room and check on her. When I got in the room, I turned on the lamp and saw that she was breathing heavy, so I called the nurse. After a few minutes, she started to gasp and I knew she was going. From that point, I knew there was nothing I could do for her. I held her hand to soothe her while she was taking her last breaths. She looked me right in the eyes and tears started running down her face and then took her last breath and went out."

"When is the funeral?"

"I'm actually on my way to the hospital to meet the fu-

neral home director, so we can make arrangements. Try to get some sleep. I will call you tomorrow when I have all the information."

After finding out the news that my grandmother just died, I could not go back to sleep. I stayed the whole night awake, crying and looking at memorable photos of her and I. I felt so bad that I was not there for her when she passed. The only thing I could think about was what if I had not driven down to see her before she passed. How guilty I would have felt. Losing my parents was different from my grandmother. Back then, I was too young to really to understand and take in all the pain. Now, that I'm older I really understand the value of life.

The next morning I got ready and went to see Dr. Whittaker unannounced. When I got there he was in his office preparing to start the day.

"Samantha. What brings you here? Did we have an appointment today", asked Dr. Whittaker.

"No. Sorry for barging in on you like this. Do you have a minute?"

"I have an appointment here shortly. What's the problem?"

"Last night my grandmother passed. As you know, she was the only one I had left. I feel like I was not there for her when she was sick like she was there for me my whole life. I knew she had been living with diabetes for several years,

but I really didn't know the effects of it. I was too busy in my own world that I forgot about everybody else. I'm so lost and confused now, that I don't know what to do."

"I'm sorry to hear that. Did you get a chance to see her before she passed?"

"Yes. I went to see her yesterday evening. When I went in the room to talk to her she was asleep, but eventually woke up. When she opened her eyes, she asked me if I were my mother and then ask me where was my father. After that she gave me, what she called, one of her heart to heart talks. Before she could finish, her eye shut again and she fell back asleep.

"There is nothing to feel guilty about. At least you got to touch her and hear her voice one last time. If you had not gotten that chance I would be able to understand your pain. We as parents know how it is to be a teenager. When I graduated from high school, I couldn't wait to get to college and be free. Once I left home I didn't go back home to visit as much as I should have and when I did I was always hanging with my old friends. This is why spending time with your children is so important because when they get older, they have no time in their; want to be busy schedule. Trust me. Your grandmother knew you loved her more than anything."

"I guess you are right."

"Did you keep your word on what you said you would

do?"

"Yes. I went out and had a good time."

"Did you make any new friends?"

"Well, I met this guy named Anthony but I lost his number."

"That's okay. The most important thing is that you got out and had a good time. Well, my eleven o'clock should be arriving any second now so we'll have to pick this up on your next visit."

"Thanks Dr. Whittaker. I needed your inspiring words. Do I owe you anything?"

"Don't be silly. No you don't owe me anything. Take care of yourself and don't be afraid to call if you need me. No matter what time it may be."

Dr. Whittaker always made me feel better when I left his office. No matter the situation, he always had a solution for the problem. I felt so comfortable talking to him. He felt more like a girlfriend whom I could discuss anything with. This was why I kept going back to him.

Since I was feeling a little better, I went to the salon and got my hair and nails done. I knew the funeral would be in a few days, so I wanted to get this part out of the way. I also needed a dress for the funeral. My next stop would be the mall. The truth is, I just needed another excuse to go shopping. As soon as I was walking out of the salon, Aunt Stacy was calling my phone.

"Hey aunt Stacy."

"Hey baby. How are you feeling?"

"I feel better. And you?"

"I'm a little on the rocky side, but I will be alright. Okay, I have all the arrangements done for the funeral service. We are not going to have it in a church because we're already having a hard time scraping up money for her casket. We are going to have a small service at the graveyard with just a few family members and friends. It will be held this Saturday at ten o'clock. Everyone will meet at grandma's house at about eight thirty and then we will leave from there."

"Ok. See you then."

After hanging up with Aunt Stacy, I went to the mall to do some shopping, other than just finding a dress for the funeral. Shopping was very therapeutic for me. Even if I wasn't buying anything, I just liked to walk around. After I finished shopping I stopped by the food court to get something to eat. While I was eating, I saw from a distance, this guy that looked like Anthony. He was talking to another girl. I didn't want to approach him. I got up and pretended as if I was heading to the restroom. When I walked passed him, I saw that it was he. He didn't notice me because he was too busy being all up in the other girls face. I can't lie. I was a little jealous at first, but what can I say? He wasn't my man.

The sun was starting to go down and I still needed to do some more studying. With graduation around the corner, this was supposed to be one of the happiest moments in my life. In a way, I envy everyone that had their parents, grandparents, sisters and brothers applauding them at graduation, while I have neither. I'm not a jealous person, but under the circumstances, I think I have the right to be.

It has been six days since my grandmother passed and now it's time for her home going service. When I arrived at her house there was a lot of people. The word had spread and a lot of people attended the funeral. I was surprised to see my grandfather's side of the family, since they never got along with her.

I was emotional. My nerves were playing tricks on me. I did not know whether I was coming or going. At about nine o'clock, the limousine arrived to escort us to the graveyard. Before we left, one of the associates gathered everyone outside to pray. Then, everyone was asked to head to his or her vehicle and turn on their headlights so they could be recognized as attendees of the funeral. When we arrived at the graveyard, the body was ready to be viewed. I sat in the front row under the tent. There were several flowers around her casket. It was a good sign and showed she was a good person and was loved by many. If not, no one would have showed up or sent flowers. That would have told a different story. I once heard a story about a man that passed. He was rude and mean to everyone he came in contact with. When he passed, everyone showed up to his funeral; not to pay respects, but to make sure he was dead.

There she was, looking so beautiful in her red dress, just as he wished. The entire time, I wished this were a prank she was playing on me. I wished she would eventually sit up and scare me half to death, but I knew that wasn't going to happen. Seeing her lying there motionless was a reality check for me. I took a whole different view on life. No more will I ever take anything or anyone for granted. I vowed to live life to the fullest, like everyday was the last. I had cried so much previously, that there were no more tears left. After the pastor spoke, I gave her one last kiss before they lowered her body into the ground. It was hard knowing that this would be my last time seeing her.

After the funeral everyone gathered back at my grandmother's house to celebrate her death. I don't know why people call it a celebration, because it's such a depressing time, when you lose someone you love. I was told once before that it was called a celebration because the person does not have to suffer anymore from all the problems of the world. Most importantly, they are now in the hands of God. I understand that, but could not find anything to celebrate about.

During the time everyone stood outside eating and talking, I locked myself in my grandmother's bedroom. I didn't want to be bothered or asked a whole lot of questions. When I got in the room, I stared at the walls and reminisced about all the nights we slept together. I used to love to sleep with her, especially when I had a nightmares or it was thundering and lightning. I used to curl myself underneath her and she would grasp me in her arms and hold me comfortably. I felt so secure that nothing in the world could have harmed me. When I laid my head on her pillow, I could smell the scent of her body. Once again, I started to cry.

Aunt Stacy noticed that I had been missing for a while, so she came in the house looking for me. When she walked in the room, I was still laying on the bed crying.

"Aw baby! Why are you beating yourself up like this?" asked aunt Stacy.

"I can't help it. I just miss her so much. When I saw her body being lowered into the ground, the reality set in. I knew it was real before, but when I actually saw it for myself, that's when I knew it was real."

"I know. It's going to be hard on all of us for a while, especially me. Everyday when I walk through those doors, I can see her face and hear her voice. Being in the house where she passed is hard enough, but now I have no one to come home to. I know you feel bad. We all do, but I'm not going to spend the rest of my day in here crying with you.

We're supposed to be celebrating. That's what she would have wanted us to do. Remember, love and let go. That was her motto."

"I will be out shortly. Just give me a few more minutes alone."

"Take your time. I'll be outside if you need me."

After Aunt Stacy left, I laid back in the bed thinking about my grandmother until I eventually fell asleep. When I woke up, everyone had gone home. I was too tired to drive back to my apartment, so I spent the night at my grandmother's house.

The next morning, I got up early and headed home. Finals started on Monday and I had not studied as much as I should have. Erica and I usually studied with each other but I haven't had much time lately. For hours, I was looking at my notes, but nothing was registering. It was so hard trying to stay focused when my mind was on my grandmother. I knew I was wasting my time, so I put all my materials away and went to see a movie. I usually fell asleep while watching movies, but this one was very good. It kept my attention. When the movie finished, I decided to go and eat some ice cream. On the way out, I saw Anthony again with a different girl. Losing his number was probably the best thing I could have done. From the looks of it, I would have been another one of his playmates. This was the problem I had with men. Instead of being honest, they play these games and think it's so cool. In my opinion, they should just say what they really want. Some women think like men. Every now and then we want the same things as they do with no strings attached. People should say exactly how they feel and sometimes you might get lucky.

When I got back home, I took a shower and watched my favorite television show. About half way through the show, it started watching me. That is, until Erica woke me up with her phone call.

"Hello."

"Hey girl. Are you sleeping?"

"Not really. I was dozing off. What's up?"

"Nothing. I just got finished studying. Did you study any?"

"I tried, however my concentration wasn't there. I couldn't get my grandmother off my mind."

"I was going to call you yesterday to see how the funeral was, but I thought it would be best if I gave you some time to yourself. How was it?"

"It was nice. She wore her red dress as she wished.

"I know you broke down."

"I didn't do that bad, but I cried 'til I couldn't squeeze out any more tears. It was really hard. Watching her slowly disappear into the ground was the roughest."

"You know I never had that grandparent experience because my dad and his parents weren't that close. It's

probably best this way because I knew I couldn't take it. I look at my dad sometimes and see him aging and I think about what I'm going to do when he's gone. Let me stop before I make myself cry. I must commend you for being so strong. I've never met anybody like you before. At an early age, you lost both of your parents and now your grandmother. I am so blessed to have you as my best friend."

"Thank you, but who said we were best friends?"

"Ooh, no you didn't. Don't do that. So did you ever talk to Anthony?"

"Girl no! I lost his number the same night he dropped me off and you called my phone. It got lost when I answered your call because I wasn't finished saving the number. I saw him last week in the mall with some girl and then today at the movies with another one. I knew he was too good to be true."

"You're not trying to marry the man. Just use him for what you need."

"I'm not you. I can't do that. I just rather not be bothered."

"You are so cranky. You should have used him to get you some so you can chill the hell out."

"Like I said before, getting laid is not going to do anything for me. So, I will se you tomorrow. Goodnight".

Erica was truly by best friend, but she was simple

minded. I hate the fact that she thought she had to use her prize possession as a tool to solve her problems.

In reality, her problems never got solved. They were just swept underneath the rug momentarily. I love myself and treasure my temple too much to just let any and everybody experience me.

After I hung up on Erica, I went straight to sleep so I could get enough rest for tomorrow's final. The next morning, I woke up two hours earlier than I normally do, so I could try to get some last minute studying in. I only got a good hour of studying in because I didn't want to stress myself out. My professors always told me not to study the day of the finals because over studying can cause you to forget. I wasn't worried too much because I always did well on my tests.

You can always tell when it is finals week because every student walks around looking so stressed and nervous. When I got to the campus, I went to the coffee shop to have a cup and a donut, and to review my notes one last time. Erica kept calling my phone, but I didn't answer because I didn't want her to say something out of hand and upset me.

The first test I took went fairly well. I felt very confident that I had done a good job. On the second exam, I wasn't as confident because I had been struggling with the class all semester long. After I finished taking my two tests for the day, I went home and kicked back for a while before studying for my next two tests. In the midst of studying, I fell asleep and slept the whole night through.

The next morning, I got up at the same time as I had done the previous morning. I took a hot shower and ate a quick breakfast before heading out. On the first test, I was a little confused. I knew I had a 50 percent chance of passing. One side of me felt confident and the other side felt the opposite. The second test was a breeze. I took the test with great comfort because math was my favorite area of study.

The third and final day of testing, I only had one final to take. After I turned in my paper, I felt this great deal of pressure relieved from my body, mind and soul. I wanted to run around the campus and scream at the top of my lungs, but it wasn't appropriate. Instead, I treated myself to a spa and a quiet dinner alone.

It would take three business days before I could find out the results of my finals. That weekend, I didn't do much besides some house cleaning and going to the gym. I was so anxious to find out the results of my finals that I couldn't sleep much. When Monday rolled around, I woke up early once again so I could get to the campus and see the results posted. I made my rounds by checking the lists according to the order in which I took the tests. After I gathered all of my grades, I started crying. It had been five long years of studying and testing, not to mention a whole lot of stress.

The only thing I wanted to do was visit the graveyard where my mother and grandmother were buried. It was great because they were buried next to each other. Before I arrived at the graveyard, I decided to stop and pick up some flowers for the both of them. As soon as I got there, it started raining, but that didn't stop me from what I came there for.

"Hey mom and grandma. I decided to drive up here and tell you the good news. I finally did it! I passed all my classes with an A, except for one that was a B. I know none of this would have been possible if it were not for the two of you doing such a good job in raising me the right way. When I was younger, what I thought were you two being hard on me wasn't hard at all. I realize now that you were molding me into the woman I am today. If you could see me now you would be so proud. I graduate this weekend with honors. I know you can't be there in flesh, but in heart, you are always with me."

Before I left Aunt Stacy surprisingly pulled up in her car. She had seen my car as she was passing by.

"Hey beanie. I didn't know you were coming up. Why didn't you not tell me?" asked Aunt Stacy.

"I wasn't planning to stay long because I have a lot to do before graduation. I just came here to share the good news with them."

"What good news?"

"I passed all my classes for graduation with honors."

With an aggressive hug she said, *"Congratulations! That is so great! So how does it feel to be the first one in the family to go to college and graduate?"*

"It's a wonderful feeling. A whole lot of work and stress was involved, but it all was worth it."

"Graduation is this weekend, right?"

"Yes, at 5 o'clock. Don't be late."

"We won't. I won't keep you. I know there is a lot you have to do, so I'll see you this weekend. Drive home safely. I love you."

"I will. I love you too."

Sometimes, taking the long way home, gives you time to think. Normally, that's what I've always done. On this trip back home, I was wondering how the worst and the best time in my life thus far could happen around the same time. Despite the fact that my vision of life was blurry at the time, I had so much to be thankful for and much more to look forward to.

The day that I had been waiting five long years for had finally arrived. I was so anxious that I didn't get much sleep the night before. A few weeks ago, I was chosen along with three other students to give a short speech at the graduation. When my grandmother passed, I declined the opportunity because I knew I would have spent most of the time crying.

The guest speaker was the mayor and one of the state

board directors of education. I sat in the front row with the other fourteen honor graduates. White was the color of the gowns for the cum laude graduates. Erica sat a few rows behind me in her blue gown. She did not graduate with honors, but she was still a really smart girl. Well, at least book smart. After everyone gave their speeches, the dean of the university gave the closing remarks. He had everyone rise and switch their tassel from the left to the right. Then, he congratulated us for being graduates and we tossed our caps in the air and cheered, "Hurray!"

All of my remaining family members came to the graduation. It was my Aunt Stacy, Uncle Tony and his wife, and all of my cousins. Usually after a big event or special occasion, families continued the celebration over a big meal whether it was at a restaurant or banquet hall. My family gathered at my apartment for dinner. Aunt Stacy had prepared all of the food the night before and cooked it at my place.

It was a good feeling to have a family gathering for the first time in years. My grandmother always said that the fastest way to the heart is through the stomach. Sharing a meal together was good for the family because it gave us time to talk and enjoy each other's company. My Uncle Tony was the clown of the family. I believe God put him on this earth to keep smiles on our faces, despite the way he lived his life. Besides, no one is perfect.

I don't think I ever laughed so hard in my life, as I did with him. We were having so much fun that we forgot about the time. Aunt Stacy had to be to work early in the morning so she had to leave. Sadly, our night had to end.

"Well, sweetie we had a wonderful time. I hate to leave, but I have to", said Aunt Stacy as she gave me a hug.

"I enjoyed you all so much. Thanks for supporting me today at the graduation."

"No problem. That's what we are here for. We have to do this again. The next time it won't be for a special occasion. So, Ms. Professional, when do you start your new job?"

"I'm supposed to start in two weeks but I probably won't. I need a little more time to relax and clear my head of all the things I have going on now."

"I understand. Don't get too relaxed and take off too long because you can start using your problems as an excuse and not go to work at all. I've seen it happen before. Remember, everything that happened in the past is done. You have to close those chapters before you begin a new one. Look at you. You're a woman now. Time flies by so fast. Don't let life pass you by. When that wave comes, you better ride it out until it disappears. Well, good luck on your job and remember to never let them see you sweat.

I'm always here if you need me."

"Thanks a lot. Your words are always encouraging."

Aunt Stacy reminded me so much of my grandmother when she was younger. I didn't want to let her go after we hugged.

"Okay, baby. Congratulations, once again, and thank you for inviting us over to share this special day with you. I can't believe I'm standing here saying these words to you. It seems like yesterday when those little skinny legs use to run around the house telling on everybody. "Gumma, dey making me fun of me." You were trying to tell on your cousins for calling you Beanie. Look at you now, a workingwoman. Let me hold something. I'm just playing, unless you really gon' give it to me. Let me stop teasing you," said Uncle Tony, as he laughed and pretended to joke with me.

I was thinking, "yeah right." If I had pulled out a dollar, he probably would have snatched my arm off along with the money.

"Don't pay him any attention with his crazy self", said Aunt Stacy.

"I'm not."

"Who asked you?" replied Uncle Tony, as he waived his hand across Aunt Stacy's face to blow her off. *"Anyways, I'm proud of you. Keep up the good work and stay focused."*

Walking out the door, the family said at the same time, "Thank you and we love you."

"I love you all too."

After they left, I took a shower and laid down. I was thinking to myself how much my life has changed. It seems like most of my life I have been depressed. There were moments in between where I found some happiness, thanks to my grandmother. Aunt Stacy was right. All of those bad things have come to pass and now it is time for me to move on and start this new chapter of my life.

Chapter 3

Briana

When the Lovinskis left the Department of Children and Family Services with Briana, a host of family and friends were gathered at the house to welcome her home. She had a couple of parents who really cared about her. From the beginning, you could see that she was going to have a good life. A least 30 family members and friends were there to share their new bundle of joy. No matter where you go or what you do there has to be a negative person around. This time that person was Danielle's father. While she was talking to her friends, he rudely interrupted their conversation.

"Danielle. Do you have a second?"

With an attitude she answered, "I guess I do now. What is it?"

"Relax. I just want to have a father to daughter talk. So, how is work?"

"Fine. Everything is going great."

"And you and Susan?"

"Okay, cut the small talk. What do you really want?"

"Well, this baby. What are you doing?"

"I'm doing something that a lot more people should do. I'm taking in a child that needs love from a real pair of parents.

"That's the point. You are not the real parent. If you want children, why don't you find a nice husband and give birth to your own. I mean, look at it. You could have at least picked a..."

"A what? White baby? My gosh. Why wasn't that a surprise? For your information I am damn pleased with my life no matter what you think of it. And yes I could have gone a adopted a white baby and have it live the American dream but color doesn't mean a thing to me or Susan."

"My goodness, Danielle. You still have a long way to go in your career. Think about what your colleagues are going to say."

"You know what I think? I think you are the reason why I don't want a man. Look at you. You are a self-centered, arrogant, egotistical bastard. And for the record, I don't give a damn what you or anybody else thinks about my life-style or me. I would appreciate it if you would stay the hell

out of my life and get the hell out of my house."

It was easy to see that Mr. Lovinski was a bigot who was raised by bigot parents. It wasn't his fault that he taught ignorance, but now he was old enough to know right from wrong. In other words, this was the way he wanted to be.

Their house was so big. It made the Henderson's house look small. Briana's room alone was about half the size of my grandmother's house. The theme of the room was suitable for a princess. She had everything from a crib to a walker. So to say, everything she needed was already set in place. The Lovinskis worked full-time, so they hired a nanny to tend to Briana. They even had her college tuition prepaid and a trust fund set up for her. This is what people would call, 'The good life.'

For Briana's fifth birthday, her parents took her to Paris. I think this was a little over the top for a five year old, but I'm speaking for a person who didn't have much. It's easy for a person with little money to say what they wouldn't do because they can't see the vision. For a person with a lot money, their thoughts and ventures are more wide spread.

When Briana was old enough to go to Pre-K, she attended private school. When she made it to the sixth grade, her parents let her transfer to a public school. She made good grades all the way through the seventh grade because she had a personal tutor. The middle school she attended was a good school until the district changed its boundaries and allowed kids from the gang-related neighborhoods to attend. In the eighth grade, her grades started to decline. Briana started hanging out with a bad group of girls that stayed in trouble. One day, Briana got caught skipping class with one of her friends. The security guard caught her behind one of the portables kissing another girl. Since they were facing a one-week suspension, they both were brought to the principal's office, where their parents were contacted and notified of the situation.

"Good afternoon. This is Principal Butler calling from Edgewood Middle School. May I speak to Ms. Lovinski?" asked Principal Butler.

"This is she. How may I help you?" replied Susan.

"I'm calling to report an issue that your daughter was involved in today. Apparently, she and another student were caught, by one of our security guards, kissing each other behind a portable."

"Did he force her to do it?"

"No ma'am. That's another issue. It wasn't a young man involved in this incident. It was another young lady. I'm sorry, but this type of action calls for a one-week suspension."

"What? I can't believe this. I understand this policy and all, but there is no need for a week suspension for kiss-

ing another girl."

"I'm sensing this doesn't bother you much. Do you know where she could have picked up or have seen such behavior before?"

"I appreciate your concern, but don't you think you are overplaying your roll?"

"My roll is to look after these children and make sure they do the right thing while they are in my care."

"Exactly. What happens on the premises; not what goes on in their personal lives is your concern. So, I would appreciate it if you would stick to your job and let me handle mine."

"That's fine. We are allowing her to finish the rest of the day in detention, but she won't be able to return to school until a week from tomorrow. Thank you for your time."

"No, thank you," said Susan, with an attitude.

Susan was so upset that she cancelled the remainder of her appointments for the day. After she hung up the phone with Principal Butler, she called Danielle.

"Good afternoon...Lovinski and Associates. How may I help you?" asked Monica, the receptionist.

"Hello, Monica. Is Danielle in her office?"

"Oh, hi Susan. Actually, she is in a meeting at the moment. Would you like for me to leave her a message or have her call you back?"

"No, that's fine. I will just talk to her when she gets home."

"Is everything ok? You sound like something is bothering you. Are you sure you don't want me to interrupt her meeting?"

"No, it's fine...really. I'll talk to her when she gets home. Thanks anyway, Monica. Take care, hun."

Monica heard the urgency in Susan's voice and decided to leave the message for Danielle anyway. When she walked in on the meeting she left a note that read, "Call Susan at your earliest convenience." Her tone sounded as if the call was urgent. Immediately, Danielle withdrew from her chair and went to her office to call Susan.

"Hello, hun. How is your day going?" said Susan when she answered the phone.

"Fine. I received your message from Monica. She said it sounded like something was wrong with you. Is everything ok?"

"I was calling to tell you that Briana was suspended from school today."

"For what and for how long?"

"We will discuss the reason when you get home, but the length of time is for a week."

"Is she with you now?"

"No. They let her finish the rest of the day in detention."

"Okay. I have to get back to this meeting. I will call

when I get out."

"Don't worry. I will see you when you get home. What time do you think you will get here?"

"Around sevenish."

"I'm going to start dinner now so it will be ready when you get here. Love you . "

"See you then. Love you, too."

Around three o'clock Briana arrived home from school. Not at all was she afraid what the consequences would be. She was more worried about what her parents and others were going to think about her.

Briana was very intelligent and respectful. The reason she hung with the wrong crowd was because of the peer pressure that was surrounding her. Who is to say how she would have ended up if her parents were not lesbians? Her parents can't take the blame her for her actions, but their lifestyle definitely had an influence on her.

When she walked in the house, Susan was in the kitchen preparing dinner.

"Hello, mom."

"Hey, honey. How was your day?"

" Well, I got in trouble today. Did Principal Butler call you?"

"As a matter of fact...she did."

"Can I explain?"

"Not at this moment. Mom will be home shortly and we

will all discuss this problem as a family. So you run up-stairs and take your shower and I will call you to come down when she gets here."

"Yes, ma'am."

Just as she hoped, Danielle arrived home at seven o'clock.

"Hey, sweetie. I'm home," announced Danielle as she walked through the door.

"How was your day?"

"It was fine. I'm just a little exhausted from all of those meeting today. Man...are they boring. I didn't do any physical work, but the mental strain of trying to stay awake is what got to me. How was your day?"

"I didn't do anything...really. When I received the call from the school, I cancelled the rest of my appointments and came home."

"So, what happened today with Briana at school?"

"Well...how can I put this? I think she is following in our footsteps."

"What do you mean?"

"Today, when I was at work, I received a call from the Principal stating that Briana and another young lady were caught kissing each other behind a portable."

"Are you serious?"

"That's the same thing I said."

"Okay. Let's gather ourselves and think about this. This

is our real test as parents. We can't fuss at her or be mad because She'll just shut us out. The only thing we can do is tell her that there are other options."

When Susan called Briana down stairs, she started getting nervous because she didn't know exactly what to say. It was her first time dealing with a situation like this. When she came down stairs, they all went into the family room to talk.

"We are going to try to discuss this without fussing. So, tell me what happened at school today," asked Danielle in a calm voice.

"Well, one of the girls I hang out with kissed me and I didn't know what to say."

"And you didn't kiss her back?"

"No. Not at first. I only kissed her because I was afraid that something would happen if I didn't."

"What did you think would happen?"

"I don't know. Maybe she would have beaten me up or something."

"What is this girl's name?"

"Shauntel."

"Are you afraid of this Shauntel?"

"A little."

"Why?"

"Because she is a bully. Almost every week she gets into a fight with a different person."

"How did you feel when she kissed you? Did you feel uncomfortable or not really?"

"It felt weird."

"Well...here is what we want to talk to you about. The fact that we are a lesbian couple may have something to do with this. I know you look up to us. Because we choose this lifestyle, does not mean you have to. I'm not going to sit here and tell the way that we are is right or wrong because who is to judge that? I honestly don't believe that homosexual people are normal as far as genetics, but we are like everyone else. The great thing about this country is that you can be anything you want to be. Don't ever be afraid to say how you feel or express yourself. If you like boys, it's perfectly fine. Only you can make that decision. We just want you to know that we are a little upset about the situation, but we still love and will always be there for you in times of need. If there is anything...I mean anything...don't be afraid to come and talk to us. If we can't help you or find an answer for you, we will definitely find someone that can," said Susan.

"Anything you want to say to us?" asked Danielle.

"No, ma'am."

"In that case...let's eat."

Briana had the coolest parents one can possibly imagine. If she had parents that were less understanding, the outcome would have been totally different. They could have gone up to that school, beat her in front of the principal and dared them to call the police. Then, they would have brought her home and beat her some more. After all of the beatings and privileges had been taken away, then they would have talked.

They ate dinner together, talked and laughed as if nothing ever happened. Dinner was the most important time of the day for them because it was when they communicated. In my opinion, it's the only time families can enjoy each other during a busy school and workweek.

During the week of Briana's suspension, Susan brought her along to work with her. Briana got to see first hand what was an everyday thing for Susan. The cool thing about it was that she got a chance to meet a lot of wealthy people and see inside these multi-million dollar homes. Susan's clientele were mostly business owners or celebrities. On one of the days, Briana got a chance to meet one of the star players from the New York Knicks and a well know model.

Across town, Danielle was working on opening another firm somewhere in the south. The areas of possibility were Georgia, one of the Carolinas, Alabama, or Kentucky. The problem was that they needed someone to head up the new location. Danielle didn't' want to do it because of two reasons. One, she was the owner and had already put in the legwork to get the company to where they were then. The other reason was, she never thought about relocating because she loved the home she helped build for the family.

Hearing the news of the new office being a possibility, Monica immediately volunteered because she always wanted to live somewhere in the south. This time was the best time to talk to Danielle because she didn't have any court appointments that day. With a light knock and a slow opening of the door, Monica said, " *Danielle. Do you have a second? I would like to talk to you about the position for the new office. I know it's still in the making but when and if this transition happens, I would like to volunteer to be transferred and help out with the opening.*"

"That's very thoughtful of you. What would we do here without you?"

"I can train someone else for a couple of weeks until they catch on. Then, I could leave."

Danielle got up from her chair and stood behind Monica with her hand on her shoulder and said, *"You have been with us so long. A lot of people around here depend on you."* In a soft voice she whispered in her ear, *"Most importantly, I need you and want you here."*

Monica quickly got up because Danielle's closeness made her feel awkward.

"Relax. Why are you so tense?"

"For one...you are married and I..."

"Don't know how you feel?"

This wasn't the first time Danielle had hit on Monica.

"Sorry for taking up too much of your time. I have to get back to work", apologized Monica as she walked out.

Danielle was an aggressive and determined person. That's why she was so successful in her business.

Several months had gone by and all of the pieces of the puzzle were starting to come together for Danielle and her new firm. Susan was still having much success in her business and Briana was doing well in school. Danielle was working so much overtime in preparation for the new location that she even worked late on Fridays. She was not going to make it home on time so she called Susan to let her know.

"Hey, honey. What time do you think you will be home?"

"I feel very exhausted, but there is so much work I still have left to do. I'm calling you...to tell you that I won't be home until later on."

"I wanted to have some 'alone time' tonight because Briana is going to sleep over one of her friends house tonight."

"Sorry, but I have a lot of work to do."

"Come home and I promise that I will help you get caught up with work this weekend. I can even help you on Monday because I'm taking the day off. Please! Can you do it for me? I'll make it extra special for you."

"I really didn't feel like working this weekend. That's why I'm staying late tonight. I promise…tomorrow we will spend the whole day together. Let me hurry. I'm not trying to get home too late. I love you. See you soon."

In a disappointing tone, she replied, *"I suppose. Bye,"* and hung up the phone.

As soon as she hung up the phone with Susan, Danielle phoned Monica.

"I plan on staying late tonight. Do you think you can work some overtime?" asked Danielle.

"Yes. I really can use the overtime."

They worked alone together until 10 p.m. Danielle kept noticing Monica gazing over at her, so she asked, "What are you planning to eat for dinner tonight?"

"I don't know. I probably will pick up something quick."

"I know a nice place to eat if you are willing to go."

"I don't know. It's getting late and…"

"Come on…have fun. It's the least I can do. I can get annoying. Don't make me beg."

"I guess it will be okay."

While Danielle and Monica were wrapping up for the night, Susan was at home getting ready to drop Briana over her friend house for the weekend. Sitting on the couch, Susan yelled upstairs to Briana, *"Are you ready?"*

"Just about."

"Don't take too long. I'm starving."

When Briana came down stairs, she could see the sad look on Susan's face.

"What's wrong?" asked Briana.

"Nothing. I'm just bored sitting here alone."

"Where is mom?"

"She had to work late again."

"On a Friday? That's not like her."

"I know. This new office is taking up all of our time together. You being gone for the weekend would have given us the quality time we have been missing. Do you want to grab a bite to eat with me before I drop you off."

"Okay."

After Danielle and Monica left the office, they headed downtown to a new restaurant on the riverfront. Monica had never been to a nice restaurant with a great ambience before so Danielle wanted to be the first to take her. Walking into the restaurant, Monica looked around in awe and said, *"This is very nice. I have never been to a restaurant that looks this nice on the outside...yet alone on the inside."*

"There is a whole lot you can miss in life if you're not connected with the right people or should I say the right person?" "Know what I mean?"

After talking over dinner, they decided to go over to the bar and have a glass of wine. Monica was not a heavy drinker. It only took two glasses to get her feeling good. When they left the bar, Danielle wanted to go for a walk along the riverfront. It seemed the more they talked, the closer they got to each other. First, they started holding hands. By the time they walked to the end of the walkway, their lips were firmly locked together. At first, Monica seemed to be bothered by the kiss. With their lips still closely together to she said, *"Wait a minute. What are we doing?"*

"It's called kissing."

"I know we are kissing but we shouldn't be. What about Susan?"

"What she doesn't know, won't hurt her. Besides, I have wanted you from the day I hired you. Why do you think I hired you with so little experience compared to the other candidates? Don't ruin the moment. Let's enjoy this moment and if you don't want to see me again I understand."

With a tight grip around Monica's waist with one hand and the other behind her neck, Danielle softly whispered in her ear, *"Do you really want me to stop?"*

"Yes...I mean no. I don't know. I'm just scared...that's all."

"There is nothing to be afraid of. I don't want to hurt you. I only want to make you feel good."

Across town, Susan and Briana were leaving the house

to go get something to eat.

"What would you like to eat?" asked Susan.

"Anything but chicken."

"We need to get something quick because I don't want to drop you off at Brandi's house too late. How does pizza sound?"

"That's fine."

When they arrived at the restaurant, both of them ordered personal sized pan pizzas with pepperoni and extra cheese. As soon as it was time to pay for the food, Susan noticed she forgot her purse in the car and had to go back and get it.

"You know what? I forgot my purse in the car. I will be right back," said Susan as she walked out the door.

"Are you serious?"

"Yes. Wait right here. I'll be back in a second."

On her way to the car she decided to take a shortcut along the waterfront. Shockingly, she saw something that crushed her heart into pieces. At the very place where she and Danielle shared their first kiss, she spotted Danielle and Monica kissing with their arms wrapped tightly around each other. They didn't see her, so she walked away quietly.

Susan was in such shock that the only thing she could do was run away and cry.

Before Susan got back to the restaurant, she dried her face

so that Briana couldn't see she had been crying. In an act of urgency, she hurried to the cash register and paid for the food.

"Hurry up! Let's go!"

"What's wrong? I thought we were going to eat here."

"I changed my mind! Let's go now!"

During the whole drive across town to Brandi's house, Susan drove in silence. Briana could tell by her facial expressions that something was wrong, but she didn't want to ask what the problem was.

"Okay. Have fun. Someone will pick you up Sunday evening."

"Thank you."

When Briana got out of the care she walked around to the driver's door and hugged her and told her, *"I love you."*

Susan was so hurt but she knew she had to keep her emotions under control. The pain was cutting so deep that she lost control of her emotions. One after the other, tears started rolling down her face. After telling Briana she loved her also, she quickly drove off.

Back at the riverfront, Danielle was getting ready to drop off Monica at home. She knew it was way past the time she should have made it home. When they arrived at Monica's place, they sat in the car and talked a few minutes more.

Rubbing softly on the back of Monica's neck, Danielle asked, *"Did you enjoy yourself?"*

"Very much so. Thank you."

"I had a great time with you this evening. What are the chances of us seeing each other again?"

"Let's not rush things. Besides, you are still in a relationship with Susan."

"I'm not trying to put a rush on you. I just find you very interesting and had to let you know before it was too late."

"Thank you. Let me give this some thought and I will get back to you."

"Whatever comes of this, I don't want it to affect our ability to work with each other. If you ever feel uncomfortable let me know."

"Sounds fair. See you on Monday. Enjoy the remainder of your weekend."

"You do the same. Good night."

As soon as Danielle pulled off, she immediately called Susan to let her know she was in route home, but Susan never answered. Danielle left a message.

"Hey hun. I'm just leaving the office. I'm on my way home now. I figured you would be asleep by the time I got home. See you soon. Love you. Bye."

Entering the garage, she noticed the fragrance of Monica's perfume on her shirt. An emergency shirt was always kept in the trunk. The only problem was that the shirt didn't match her pants and Susan saw the shirt she had on when she left the house to go to work.

As soon as Susan heard the garage door lift, she ran down stairs to the entertainment room to pretend she as if she was watching television.

When Danielle entered the house, she sat her bag by the door and walked towards the entertainment room. She could see the glare from the television on the walls. As soon as she turned the corner, she saw Susan laid out on the couch.

"Hey honey. I called you about fifteen minutes ago. Did you not hear the phone ring?"

Very shortly, she replied, *"I heard it."*

"What's wrong with you? You're not upset because I had to work late, are you?"

"Oh nothing. I'm fine. What happened to your shirt?"

"A coffee spill. I was drinking a cup at my desk and accidentally spilled some on my shirt."

"What took you so long?"

"I had tons of paper work to complete before Monday. I'm sorry. I know this was supposed to be our weekend alone. I will make it up to you."

"Did you eat anything?"

"Yes. I'm full..."

Before she could get out another word, Susan cut her off,

"Of sh_t or should I say from Monica's saliva? I saw you tonight."

"What are you talking about?"

"Don't play stupid with me. You know exactly what I'm talking about. How could you after all we have been through?"

"I don't know what you are talking about."

"You can't even look me in the face. I have given you sixteen years of my life. The least you can do is be honest with me."

Danielle stood there and would not answer. After a long pause, Susan said, "*Fine. I'm leaving.*"

When Susan got up to leave, Danielle grabbed her by the arm to stop her.

"Okay...wait."

She sighed heavily with her head down and began talking.

"Let me explain."

"I'm listening."

"First, let me start off by saying sorry. I take all the blame for this. Monica didn't come on to me...I came on to her."

"How long has this been going on?"

"This was the first time we went out."

"So...you are telling me that this overloaded with work stuff was all a lie?"

"No. We worked late. I offered to take her to dinner since I asked her to stay on a last minute notice. We went to

the riverfront to eat, had a few drinks, and one thing led to another. I'm so sorry. It will never happen again."

"How am I supposed to trust you after this? How can I be sure that this will never happen again?"

"It won't. I give you my word."

"Obviously, your word has proven to be tainted. I'm sitting here asking myself has our relationship been a lie all this time?"

"Don't go that far. You know I love you very much. I made a mistake like anyone could."

"I don't know. I need some time to think about this. I'm not staying here tonight. I can't. I'm going to get a room somewhere for a few days and think this whole thing over. If I choose to come back I will. If not, I will let you know."

As Susan was trying to walk away, Danielle stopped her again.

"Why do you have to leave? I mean..."

"The best thing you can do right now is let me go. If you care for me as much as you say you do, let me go."

Danielle released Susan's arm so she could leave. In two black suitcases, Susan had already packed some of her clothes before Danielle got home. As she was walking out the door, she said, *"Don't forget to go and pick up Briana Sunday evening. I guess you got what you want now."*

Without giving Danielle a chance to reply, she slammed the door and sped off in her car.

For the rest of the weekend, Susan stayed in a hotel about an hour outside of town so that Danielle couldn't come looking for her.

That night, Danielle didn't sleep a wink. Without Susan in the house, Danielle felt lost. For the past sixteen years, Susan was all she knew. Through all those years, they got to know each others likes and dislikes, up and downs, and in and outs. Most people are afraid to step outside of the box because it makes them leave their comfort zone. Even though Danielle was being unfaithful, her comfort zone was with Susan. Sometimes, getting too comfortable with someone can be a bad thing, because you tend to forget about the things you used to do in the beginning. After a while, things begin to disappear and you don't put in as much effort to show that someone how much you still care for them. It is selfish to think that your companion will never leave.

When Sunday rolled around and it was time to pick up Briana from her friends house, Danielle was nervous because she wasn't prepared to answer any questions about Susan that Briana might ask.

As soon as she pulled into Brandi's driveway, Briana was walking out to meet her. Just as she expected, the first thing she said was, *"Hey mom! Where is mom?"*

"She will be away for a few days. How was your weekend?"

"Actually, it was pretty good. I had a lot of fun. Is she gone on a business trip?

"No. It was for personal reasons."

Just as fast as Danielle tried to change the subject, Briana would bring it back.

"*When is she coming back*?"

"*Hopefully soon.*"

Briana loved both of her parents, but as you can see she was more attached to Susan. She was more of the mother figure because she played the more feminine roll in the relationship.

When they arrived home, Danielle immediately ordered Briana to go upstairs and take a shower to avoid any more questions.

Two days had passed and no one had heard from Susan. Danielle's worry was more over whom she was with rather than if everything was ok. Her actions remind me somewhat of a man. I guess this was the reason she was the more masculine one in the relationship.

One week from the day she left, Susan came back home for several reasons. One reason being she missed Briana. She also missed her bed and hated the fact that she was paying a mortgage on a house where she wasn't even laying her head. The main reason was even though she was disappointed with Danielle…she loved her to death.

It was about eleven o'clock when she walked through

the door. Danielle was in the entertainment room sleeping on the couch. For a few minutes, she sat on the edge of the couch starring at Danielle and thinking of a million reasons to leave again, but couldn't find one. She then went upstairs to Briana's room and kissed her on the forehead while she was sleeping. When she came back down stairs to sit back on the edge of the couch, Danielle felt the movement and woke up. In great surprise, she jumped up and said, *"Hey, honey! How long have you been here?"*

"About ten minutes. How are you?"

"Fine...now that you are here. You?"

"I would be doing better if everything between us were back to normal. How do we get back there?"

"I know I made the biggest mistake of my life and I'm sorry. You are more than anything I could have ever wished for. Repairing us is going to take time and I'm willing to prove my love for you."

"I want to believe you, but it's so hard right now. The only way I could see myself back with you, in peace of mind, is that you have to get rid of Monica or we make the move down south to start the new office. The thought of you going to work everyday seeing the woman you cheated with doesn't sit well with me and is going to cause a major problem between us."

"Why do you have to give me an ultimatum of such magnitude? I don't want to get rid of Monica because of a

mistake I made. She is a very good worker and shouldn't be punished on my behalf."

"I don't care about what is best for her. You should have thought about that before you did it. It's either her or me. You make your choice."

"Of course, I choose you. Can you at least give me some time to figure this out?"

"You have two days to figure it out or I'll be out."

"Let's just go to bed and we'll discuss this tomorrow."

With an emotional hug, they kissed each other and went to bed.

The next morning, Danielle woke up early to think about how she was going to handle the situation that was at hand. Firing Monica would hurt her deeply, but losing Susan would cut deeper. After contemplating for hours, she finally made a decision that would be best for everyone. In the afternoon board meeting, she informed everyone of her decision. *"For weeks we have been looking for someone to head up the new office. Unfortunately we haven't been that successful. After discussing it with my family, I have made the decision to head up the office myself. For all of you that I have shared so many pleasant years with, I appreciate the memories we have together. To the people that haven't been here so long...thank you for all the hard work you have done. It's a sad moment for me, but I have to move on. Next week, our house will go on the market for sale. As soon as it is sold, we will be moving on. Again, thank you all for the great times together and remember just because I'm leaving doesn't mean you have lost a friend. I will always be only a call away."*

After breaking the news to everyone, Danielle felt really good about her decision. On the way home, she stopped by the shopping center to pick up some flowers and a bottle of wine to celebrate with Susan. When she walked through the garage door, the ray of light could be seen coming from her smile. Susan was in the kitchen cooking and Briana was doing her homework on the bar top.

"Hello. What are you so happy about?" asked Susan.

"I did it. I made the decision for us to leave. I informed everyone today in our meeting."

"That was fast."

The whole time they were talking, Briana had this curious look on her face. They knew they would eventually have to break the news to Briana, so they told her right then.

"Briana, as you may know mommy is trying to open another office down south. We were looking for someone to move down and get the office up and running, but couldn't find a person we were comfortable with, so Susan and I made the decision to move down there and do it ourselves. I know this is a shock for you right now, but I promise it will all work out for the best for the three of us. How do you feel

about that?"

"I don't know. All of my friends are here. What is it like where we are moving?"

"I have to be honest with you. That part we don't know yet. We are going to plan a trip for all of us to go down there soon and check out some different neighborhoods. We promise to let you have a say in the choice. Fair enough?"

"I guess."

After dinner, they sat around and watched television until it was time to go to bed.

Chapter 4

Riana

Riana's farewell wasn't as exciting. When Stephanie and Frank reached the car, their argument resurfaced because of Frank's nonchalant attitude. Instead of going home and welcoming the baby, Stephanie had Frank drop her off at her mother's house. Before the car could come to a complete stop, she got out and grabbed Riana. Slamming the door closed, she angrily said, *"You don't have to pick me up. I will find a way home."*

"Cool with me," he replied before speeding off like a mad man.

Looking on from the front porch was Stephanie's mother, Linda.

"I see you two at it again," giggled Linda.

"Not now momma," said Stephanie in frustration.

"So is this grandma's new baby? Look at her. She is so precious...and these cheeks, I want to bite them. Now, you know this is a huge responsibility."

"I know. You won't let me forget."

"This isn't one of those baby dolls you used to play with. This is the real deal. You never did your dolls hair or changed them. I hope you are better with this one than you were with those dolls. Let me set some rules. I don't mind babysitting sometimes, but don't make it a habit. My days of raising children are over. Other than that, we are good. Now, tell me what is wrong with Frank."

"I don't know. He just started acting funny when we went to pick up Riana. I asked him what his problem was and the argument started from there."

"Do you think it was because of the baby?"

"I don't think so. We talked about adopting a long time before we did it because we knew he couldn't have children."

"Sometimes people say things they really do not mean or feel just to make the other person happy. I can somewhat understand how he feels. Every man wants that little boy that they can raise to be like them. When they can't, it's a hurting feeling. Give him some time. He will come around."

"I hope so. This is his responsibility just as much as it

is mine."

"Let me ask you something. If you and Frank were to ever get a divorce...God forbid you do...who do you think is going to have to take care of that baby all by themselves?"

" Me."

"Exactly! So don't worry about that. You have to do what's best for you and this baby. Hell, seventy-five percent of guys aren't around to do anything for their children anyway. I got to be honest. There were a lot of times I felt like throwing in the towel and saying forget everything and everybody, but I knew you children depended on me. I prayed and kept faith in God and He guided me along the way. You will be fine. Now, let's go in and eat. Besides, these bugs are getting on my last nerve."

After dinner, Linda dropped them off at home.

"Thanks for the ride, momma."

"No problem. Drop by sometime and let me spend some time with my grandbaby. Love you."

"I will. Thanks again. Love you too."

Stephanie knew Frank wouldn't be home because every time they had an argument he left and didn't come home until late at night. She and the baby went inside to get ready for bed. While giving Riana a bath, Stephanie started talking to her sweetly.

"Welcome home! This is where we are going to spend

so many years together. All of your birthdays and sleep-overs will take place right here...unless I hit the lottery. We are going to have so much fun together. I can't wait until I can take you to the park, do your hair, and most importantly, go shopping with you."

After giving her a bath, Stephanie put her to sleep in her newly decorated pink and white room. She then took a shower herself and went to bed. About 1:30 in the morning Frank came stumbling in the house as usual. When he got in the room he took off all of his clothes and laid on top of Stephanie. She did not want to be bothered so she rolled over and turned the opposite way. Frank was not a quitter, so he kept on rubbing on her and kissing on her neck to arouse her. After a few minutes of trying to fight him off, she finally gave in. The smell of alcohol did not turn her on in the least, but she loved his aggressiveness. Frank wasn't in the streets anymore, but he still had that thug mentality when it came to sex. This was the reason why she was so far gone over him. I guess, after all, good girls do love bad guys.

I, personally, never understood why women loved a roughneck, pants sagging, Timberland wearing thug until I had my own encounter with one. You see, thugs are far more different than your average gentleman. You can't plan a life with a thug because there are too many unknowns. If you like to plan, then put a gentleman into play.

If you need a backbreaking experience, you call a thug because everything about him is rough. I also found, with a thug you can let your hair down and just be yourself. It's hard sometimes to do that with a gentleman because you feel like you have to watch what you do and say. Therefore, my preference is a man who takes care of his business and knows how and when to turn the thug on and off.

The next morning they woke up early to eat breakfast before leaving for church. Every Sunday was a fight trying to convince Frank to come to church. His mother wasn't a very religious person, so he didn't grow up with Christian beliefs as Stephanie had. The church they attended was named Mount Calvary Temple of Worship. The pastor was a famous one. All of his services were televised. He wrote books and traveled the world teaching the gospel as a motivational speaker. The church held close to five thousand people and every Sunday was seated to its capacity.

Stephanie joined the church because her best friend, Kimberly, had been a member for several years. Prior to adopting Riana, they made the decision to make Kimberly the Godmother. She didn't have a Godfather because Kimberly was single and Frank didn't have any stable friends that they could imagine taking on that roll. That particular Sunday was the day of the Christening. It was an emotional experience for Stephanie because the reality of her becoming a fulltime mother had set in.

Afterward, both Kimberly's and Stephanie's family gathered at Kimberly's house to celebrate. Like usual, when a new baby was brought into the family, they passed it around for each person to give their blessings. Stephanie received gifts that she had previously purchased. Riana's room was equipped with everything she needed. Her mother always taught her that when someone gives you a gift, you accept it anyway even if you don't need it or can't use it. Stephanie didn't want to be rude, but made an announcement anyway.

"On behalf of Riana, Frank, and I, we would like to thank each and every one of you for coming and showing your support. As some of you may know, Frank and I couldn't bare children on our own, so this is why we made the choice to adopt. I appreciate your hospitality and the gifts, but unfortunately we already have most of these gifts. If you can be so kind as to return them and exchange them for pampers and formula, we would greatly appreciate it. I emphasize on pampers and formula because they cost so much and babies run through them so fast. We can never have too much of either. Thank you all again and enjoy the rest of your evening."

She knew that making that announcement would have unintentionally upset someone and they would return the gifts and pocket the money.

Stephanie took a leave of absence from her job for two

months, so she could stay home and take care of the baby. Frank pretended to be okay with it, but the look on his face every morning when he had to be up for work at five o'clock, while Stephanie slept peacefully, told another story. It took a little while for him to come around, just as her mother had said.

When Riana turned one year old, they gave her, her first birthday party at the house. A host of family and friends attended the party. When it was time to cut the cake, Frank dunked her face into the cake. It was a memorable moment for the Johnsons.

Years passed and Frank was steadily climbing the corporate ladder. Stephanie had changed jobs a few times trying to make a better salary and Riana had started elementary school and was doing very well. The neighborhood in which they lived had gotten worse due to gang violence. Stephanie wanted to move because she felt that it wasn't a safe environment to raise a kid. Frank didn't feel the need to move because he felt safe due to his old street reputation. Sometimes, when they would be sitting on the front porch some of the young bangers would come by and chat with Frank. They would be laughing and showing off their guns. Stephanie did not like it because it seemed like if he was cool with their gang involvement. She never heard him try to tell them something positive and that bothered her. When he finished talking to them, she asked him, *"Why do you encourage them? Shouldn't you be a roll model to them and show them there are better things in life than what they are doing now?"*

"I'm not encouraging them. No matter what I say, they are going to do it anyway. You should know how it works. Once you join, there is no way out, except through death."

"You got out and nothing happened to you."

"Yeah...Well, maybe I was one of the lucky ones."

"You know...you have such a bad attitude about certain things. What if that was your kid? If Riana joined a gang, what would you say to her?"

"If she was under age, of course I would talk to her but if she was eighteen there's nothing I could tell her because she's going to do what she want to do no matter what we say to her. Besides, I'm not those kids father. Hell, their parents can't even control them and you think I can? As far as a roll model, I never said I wanted anybody to look up to me. What am I doing that's so good in my life that someone would want to look up to me for? Man...I'm a construction worker, not some famous celebrity."

As he was walking past her into the house, he started mumbling to himself.

"Roll model. Who the hell she thinks I am? Sidney Poitier or somebody?"

The next day Stephanie received a call from the Department of Children and Family Services. It was Ms. Anderson calling to do a routine check up on Riana. Every so often, the adopting parents receive phone calls and inspections of the homes to make sure the children are still in a safe and clean environment. When the phone rang, Stephanie was getting out of the shower. She ran to the phone and picked it up before the answering machine came on. In a heavy breathing tone, she spoke, *"Hello."*

"Good evening, Mrs. Johnson. How are you today?"

"I'm fine and yourself?"

"Did I catch you at a bad time?"

"No, not at all. I ran to the phone and now I'm out of breath, but everything is okay."

"As you know, I'm just calling to do my routine check-up. How is she doing?"

"She is doing excellent. Her grades are very good and she's growing fast."

"And yourself?"

"I'm doing wonderful, also. I just started a new job that I'm finally completely happy with, so everything is going well."

"That's wonderful. I won't keep you. I have a few more calls to make. Well, you all take care and call me if anything changes."

"I certainly will. Enjoy the rest of your day. Bye."

"You do the same. Bye."

Ms. Anderson was a very sweet woman. She went above and beyond her job. She made sure the children she gave away to foster parents were taken care of. Most people do their job just because they have to, but she did it because that was what she always wanted to do. Most importantly, she loved children and hated to see them mistreated.

A couple more years had gone by and Riana was in middle school. Her grades were still good, but they took a slight decline. The middle school she attended had a terrible educational program. They couldn't get any good teachers to stay because they were afraid of the gang activity. The school reminded me much of the movie "Lean on Me," but with no Joe Johnson. It was out of control. The principal was an African American male that didn't care what went on at the school. His actions showed it. The school board could have done more to change it, but they didn't care much about the future of the children in the low poverty schools either. All of their funds and resources went to better the education of the children in the suburban schools.

Just across the street was the high school Riana would be attending the following year. This school was even more out of control. The campus police patrolled both schools 24 hours a day. Each entrance of the schools was equipped with metal detectors and an officer who patted each student down before they could enter the building. Almost every week, there was a stabbing or shooting reported near the school.

For some reason, Riana was not afraid of the environment she was living in. As a matter of fact, she was very curious to see what the lifestyle of a gangster was like. In the eighth grade, she started to hang out with the 21st street gang. It took no time for her to head in the wrong direction. From the beginning of the school year, she started to skip classes and hang out in the bathrooms and hallways…if she came to school at all. Since Stephanie and Frank got home late, Riana had enough time to throw away mail and delete the messages her teachers left on the answering machine about her attendance and grades. Every time Stephanie would ask about her day, she would lie and make it seem as if it was productive. Stephanie never checked her work because she thought she could trust her to ask for help if needed.

Both Frank and Stephanie started noticing changes in her…from her dress code to her appearance. Some days Riana would come home with different scars on her body. When asked about them she would lie.

"How was school today," asked Stephanie.

"It was fine."

"What happened to your face?"

"I got in a fight with this girl after school."

"For what?"

"I don't know. She was just talking a whole lot of junk to me and when she came too close I hit her."

"I'm sorry you have to go through all of this just to get an education. If things get worse, we might have to use grandma's address and transfer you to another school."

"No! You don't have to do that. I'll be okay...I can handle myself."

"Do you need dad or I to come down to the school and talk to the police officer about this problem?"

"No. I'm fine. I promise."

The following week, she came home with a broken nose…the same week report cards were scheduled to be sent home. Riana did not tell Stephanie because she knew there would be a whole lot of questions asked and she was running out of lies to tell. The only way she found out was by going in Riana's room and discovering blood on her pillow the next morning while waking her up for school. When she looked in her face she could see her nose was slightly leaning to the left. She asked Riana what happened and again she told another lie. Instead of letting her go to school, she took her to the hospital. After waiting in the emergency room for over three hours, they were finally called to the back to take an x-ray. While viewing the x-ray, the doctor saw that her nose was broken in two places. Since there was no surgery required, the doctor put a bandage over her nose and gave her instructions to be careful.

After leaving the hospital, Stephanie went up to the school to talk to the principal. When she got there the school was on lockdown due to a drive bye shooting. No one could leave or come inside the building. Stephanie decided to take the rest of the day off with Riana. When they got home, Riana went to sleep on the couch because the pain relievers made her drowsy.

While she was sleeping, Stephanie thought it would be a good idea to clean the house and do laundry because she didn't get a chance the past weekend. She started in Riana's room because she wanted to wash the bloodstains from her pillow. As soon as she pulled off the sheets, a book fell to the floor. When she picked it up, she saw that it was a diary. Her first thought was not to look in it because she wanted to respect her privacy. Her second thought was to read it because of Riana's strange behavior lately. When she opened it there was a blue scarf and a pictures of Riana, some gang affiliates, and her report card. The few pages that she read were startling. She read about how Riana lost her virginity and some of the things she had to do in order to join the gang. Stephanie was so heartbroken. The level of trust she had for her had been broken. Nothing was said to her until Frank got home from work. When she told Frank what happened, his response wasn't as caring as she thought it should have been. Stephanie couldn't wait until after dinner to discuss the issue with Riana. In an angry tone, she called her down stairs, *"Riana."*

Looking down over the staircase, she answered in a respectful manner. She knew something was wrong.

"Yes ma'am?"

"Come down those stairs right now. Can you explain all of this"?

Riana didn't have an answer because she knew she was busted.

"I trusted you and this is how you repay me...right? What the hell were you thinking about? I told you to stay away from those hoodlums and you go and do the opposite."

She then looked towards Frank and said, *"I told you this was not a good neighborhood to raise children."*

Frank quickly got upset and stood up and replied, *"Why are you putting the blame on me? I'm not the one out there getting in trouble."*

She then looked back at Riana and asked, *"Don't you have anything to say? I'm waiting."*

"I'm sorry."

"You're sorry...that's it? I tell you what...Monday I'm going down to that school to withdraw you. I refuse to let my parenting go down the drain. Even worse...I'm not ready to go to any more funerals 'cause that's what's go-

ing to happen. Either death or prison…that's the only thing that comes from gang banging."

Before she walked out of the room, she looked at Frank in frustration and said, *"You better talk to her because you know that life better than I do. Tell her about all the things you had to go through because of the bad decisions you made."*

When she walked out of the room, Frank sat Riana down and talked to her.

"You know, you really hurt her. She trusted you so much."

"What about you?"

"Well, I understand what you are going through. I'm not taking sides with you because what you are doing is not safe, but I can relate. You don't have a clue what you are getting yourself into. That life you're trying to live is so much more than the eye can see."

"So, you have been in a gang, too?"

"Yeah. I'm not proud of it, but I have been."

"Which one?"

Smiling, he answered, *"The same one you're in. Of course, that was a long time ago. Things were way different then. When I was out there, it wasn't as bad as it is now. We didn't have so many young ones in the gang because the leaders wouldn't allow it. Now a days, it seem like they come out of the womb throwing up signs. How do you feel about gang banging?"*

"I don't know. I haven't done anything bad yet. The worst part was the initiation. Me against six people wasn't fun."

"I know what you mean", he said with a little laugh because he could relate.

"You know mom is not going to allow you to stay here and still be in that gang? Either you get it together, or you get gone."

After a long pause, she asked, *"How am I supposed to change? Remember...once you're in, there is no getting out?"*

"Yeah. I quickly forgot that part. Let me see what I can do."

The next day after work, Frank went to the old neighborhood where he first started banging. When he pulled up to the abandoned house where the gang hangs and pushes their drugs, there were four watch outs in front of the house. When he got out of the car, all four of the boys raised their handguns and one of them said, *"You better announce yourself unless you wanna get blasted."*

With his hands in the air he replied, *"My name is Frank. I am not here for trouble. I'm looking for the man in charge."*

"For what? He ain't accepting no visitors."

"I just want to talk at him for a few minutes...that's

all."

"You better raise up. That's all you got is a minute to bounce before I blast you out of here."

Looking on from the window, Lil Jay stepped outside and asked Frank, *"What's on your mind?"*

"My name is Frank..."

Before he could finish saying his name, Lil Jay finished it for him, *"Johnson. I know who you are. You one of the brothers that helped start this set."*

Looking at the gang member with the gun pointed at Frank, he told him, *"Let him pass. He's cool. As a matter of fact...ya'll pay some respect."*

Together, all the boys threw up their brotherhood sign to show respect for him. Lil Jay then brought him in the house to discuss whatever it was that Frank wanted.

"What's the problem?"

"I'm going to make this short and quick. I need for you to let my daughter out of your gang."

"I'm not going to bother to ask her name because that doesn't matter. You know how the game goes. Once you become a banger...you're always a banger."

"I know but I need for you to make some exceptions this time."

"What's so special about this one? Obviously, you're doing something wrong. That's why she came to me."

"I think this was more of a peer pressure thing."

"It ain't that much pressure in the world. Most people do stuff because they want to do them. Then they come up with excuses to justify the reasons for their actions. Besides, she's a girl. We didn't put a gun to her head and make her join. She joined on her own."

"What will it take to for us to settle this?"

"I don't know. I pretty much have everything I need already. I tell you what...let me think about it and I'll find you."

In a sarcastic tone, Frank replied, *"Yeah...I'll be waiting."*

On the way home, he was thinking of the best way to tell Stephanie that the conversation didn't go as smoothly as he had expected. Even though Lil Jay said he would think about it, Frank knew the answer was no.

When he pulled into the parking lot Stephanie and Riana were sitting on the front porch waiting for him.

"Hi, daddy", said Riana.

"What happened," asked Stephanie without greeting him.

In a sarcastic way, he replied, *"Oh, my day was fine and yours?"*

"I'm sorry. I was just interested to find out what the outcome was. Did you talk to him?"

"Yeah. We talked for a minute. I don't think I really

got anywhere with him, but I tried."

"What did he say?"

"He said what every banger would say. Once you join, there is no getting out."

With an upset look on her face, Stephanie got a little loud and said, *"What happened to this so-called "street credibility" you're supposed to have?"*

In return, he shouted, *"Wait a minute."*

He looked at Riana and asked, *"Can you go inside and wait for me? I'll be in there in a few minutes."*

Frank waited a few seconds until Riana got in the house before he finished saying what he had to say.

"First of all, let me get one damn thing straight with you right now. You ain't going to keep coming at me the way you do. I'm known and respected by plenty of people. Times have changed. These new kids don't want to hear nothing I got to say. The only thing they want is money and blood and I'll be damn if I'm going to let them have mine over this. Hell, most of the guys I used to run with are either in prison or dead. It's only a few of them left. When I need something, I go to the sources I know. So, don't sit there and blame me. I didn't get us into this mess. If you don't have anything else better to say, I'm going in the house."

After he finished checking Stephanie, he went upstairs to talk to Riana. When he got up there, her room door was closed. Through all the distrust, he still didn't want to invade her privacy. He knocked on the door and announced himself.

"Riana. It's me. Can I come in?"

"Come in. It's open."

"How was your day?"

"It was good and yours?"

"Very stressful...mentally and physically. I stopped by and talked to Lil Jay, but I don't think it got me anywhere. This is something you are going to have to deal with. I advise you to try and stay away from them. If that doesn't work, maybe we will have to take another route."

"How can I dodge them when they are everywhere I go?"

"That is something you are going to have to figure out. You got your self into this situation...try to get your self out."

When Frank left the room, Riana sat on her bed thinking of all the things he told her. She knew she had to make a decision. It was either make Stephanie and Frank happy or continue down that road of destruction.

Riana was afraid to return to school because she knew it would be tough avoiding the members of her set. Fortunately, no one bothered her or said a word to her again. Lil Jay had given the word to let her free because of the respect he had for Frank and he couldn't make any money off of her.

For the remainder of her eighth grade year, she brought her grades back up and graduated on the B honor roll. Stephanie and Frank's relationship had been on shaky ground for a couple of months and was getting no better.

The summer after completing the eighth grade, Riana went to summer school so she would be ahead when regular school began again.

After a few months of arguing and fighting, Stephanie and Frank were thinking of getting a divorce. He was so stressed over their relationship that it started to take toll on his job. The stress was bothering him so much that he couldn't perform his daily duties.

Most people can relate to what he felt because we have all been in that position before. I know how it felt because I went through it with my first love. When you go through these changes, your mind and body plays tricks on you. You can't eat or sleep. Your nerves bother you so much that your stomach gets upset and you don't know whether you are going left or right or have to…you know what I mean.

One evening when he got home from work he wanted to talk to her to discuss the future of their relationship. When he walked in the house, she was on the phone, as usual, with one of her girlfriends. As time went on, their relationship became less communicative. This was the reason she claimed to be on the phone so much. Frank, on the other hand, took his frustrations out in other ways. He either locked himself in the guest room or hung out all night drinking with the fellows. On this night, he didn't feel like either. Instead, he walked over to her and asked, *"Can you get off the phone for a minute?"*

In her nonchalant mood, she answered, "For what?"

"Because we need to talk."

With a long pause and sigh, she said to her girlfriend on the phone, *"Girl, give me a minute. I'll call you right back."*

After she hung up the phone, she looked at Frank in disgust.

"What's up?"

"What's up with the attitude?"

" I don't have one, baby."

"You do have an attitude. It's written all over your face. This is the problem. Every time I try to talk to you...the only thing you give me is an attitude."

"Well, maybe I do have a little attitude. Now, you see how it feels to be on the other end of the stick. I thought you said you had something you wanted to talk about. I'm not about to sit here and waist my time discussing my attitude."

The expression on Frank's face could have been a Polaroid moment. The problem with most guys is that they walk around with this "whatever" type attitude and treat the person they are supposed to love like trash. When the woman gets fed up and gives him a dose of his own medicine, he can't handle it. This is when they want to try to work things out, but it's too late. A woman scorned is a dangerous woman. When she gets fed up, there is nothing a man can do about it.

Instead of arguing back and forth, he calmed down and started talking to her in a respectful manner.

"I'm not trying to argue with you, so I'll get to the point. What is the problem with us?"

Still with an attitude, she answered, *"I don't know. You tell me."*

"The only thing we do now is argue. It has been weeks since we last touched each other."

"It's funny you said that because that's the only time I can get you to show some affection. If it was not for that, I probably wouldn't exist."

"It's not that way. Lately, I just have been feeling depressed lately. So instead of taking it out on you, I stay to myself."

"That's understandable. Everyone has those days when they need some time to themselves, but the way you handle things don't make matters any better."

"I know. That's why I can truly say I'm sorry."

"What are your reasons for being depressed?"

"A lot of things. This job is stressing me out, all of the problems we're having, and this responsibility of raising a kid."

"What do you mean?"

"I mean I never wanted to adopt any children. Once I knew I couldn't make any of my own, I completely erased the thought of children from my mind. I said yes to adopting because I knew you wanted children and I wanted to see you happy. I know I'm not a good father to Riana and it shows because it's hard for me to put on this front when it's something that I really don't want to do. I love her, but this parent thing is something I'm just not ready for."

"Wow! That comment is hard to swallow. So basically, this whole time you have been living a lie."

Getting more frustrated, she started mocking his old sayings,

"I love you. I can't wait until you have my baby. It's ok, we can adopt. Whatever it takes to make you happy. I bet a lot more things in this relationship have been a lies."

"You see? Every time I try to talk to you this is what I get. I just don't know what to do anymore. Maybe we should just take a break from each other. You and Riana can stay here and I'll leave."

"Yes. That's sounds good to me. I think that would be best for all of us."

Listening upstairs through the cracked door, Riana

heard the entire conversation. She was hurt to hear they were breaking up, but the worst pain came from Frank's words about parenting. She had tried so hard to change the direction she was heading in life by getting out of the gang because she thought it would have brought them closer as a family. Now that Frank was leaving, she felt like it was a waist of time.

After arguing with Stephanie, Frank left the house in anger, knowing he didn't have anywhere to go. Like most men, he spoke faster than his brain could function. Driving around and thinking to himself, he decided to stop by a bar and have a few drinks. While downing a few shots, a man walked up to him and asked his name.

"Excuse me, sir. Would your name be Frank?"

"It depends on who wants to know."

"The owner says he know you and would like to talk to you."

"No. I think you have the wrong guy."

Pulling his coat jacket to the side to expose his gun, the man then said, *"Sir, please come with me. I won't ask anymore."*

Frank saw the gun and without hesitation he got up from his seat and followed the man to the back of the bar. When he got in there, he saw Mr. B. He was the guy who introduced him to the hard knock life. Everything he learned came from him. When Frank was a petty hustler,

Mr. B showed him how to get real money. Frank had much respect for him because he was much like the father he never had.

The room was full of monitors that were viewing the entire interior and exterior of the bar. This was how he was spotted at the bar. Smoking a cigar behind his desk, Mr. B ordered Frank to take a seat.

"Frankie! It's been a long time since we've seen each other. How have you been?"

"I'm ok. Just working...trying to get by, you know."

"I missed you kid. What happened? Did you forget about me? Remember those days when I showed you the ropes? Those were the good times and now look at you. You're supposed to have a piece of my pie. I always looked at you as a son. Come work for me for old time sake. It will be different this time. I need a partner. This old man is getting tired. It's almost time that I hand the business over to someone that I can rely on. What do you say?

"I'll pass. Look, I would love to sit around and reminisce with you, but I have to get going. So I'll see you..."

As he was trying to get up, Mr. B's right hand man Orvy pressed down on his shoulder to make him sit down. Mr. B then got up from his chair and went and sat on the corner of his desk next to Frank and said, *"Look here. I know you're trying to be a family man and all and do the right thing, but the truth is you belong out here where you started. Look at you...you're too smart for that. I tell you what. Let's say you give it some thought and get back to me."*

Mr. B reached in his coat pocket and pulled out a few hundred dollar bills and tried to hand them to him. Frank was getting very annoyed by Mr. B's bribing after he already told him no.

"I appreciate your gesture, but I don't want any part of this life anymore and I don't need your money. Now, can I go?"

When Frank said what he had to say, he tossed the money back at Mr. B. Just, as one of his bodyguards was about to make a move on Frank, Mr. B waived him off.

"Wait. It's fine. You know that hurt my feelings. I show my appreciation for you and you throw money back at me. You better thank God I see you as a son or else."

He then looked at his men and said, *"He can go now."*

When Frank got up out of his chair, Orvy tried to hand him the money again and Frank threw both arms in the air to reject it once again. Before Frank could exit the room, Mr. B said, *"The offer still stands if you change your mind. And the drinks are on me."*

He did not want to stay a minute longer. Despite Mr. B's offer, he paid his tab anyway and quickly left the bar.

He was so confused at this point in his life that he didn't know what to do. Several times he thought about taking up the offer Mr. B approached him with, but he knew the risk was too dangerous. For the next few weeks, he lived in the guesthouse of his long time friend Xavier. Xavier was married with two children and used to run the streets with Frank when they were in the gang. Frank was the reason why he was respected on the streets because everyone knew they rolled with Mr. B. Even as a kid, Frank was Mr. B's main hustler.

Frank and Stephanie made several attempts to patch up their relationship. It seemed like the more they tried, the worse it got. Finally, they made the decision to separate for a while. Their separation was so long that there was talk of divorce. Frank already knew that would not happen because he was not going to sign the papers.

Back at the house, Stephanie and Riana were trying to adjust to Frank's absence. Stephanie knew that something was wrong with Riana by the way she moped around the house. Riana never told Stephanie that she overheard Frank talking about his dislikes of parenting and how it really broke her heart.

Inside the house there was a cold feeling. The air was absent of love. Even though there was a lot of arguing, the house felt warmer when Frank was around. Despite their wrongdoing, the only true love Riana felt was from her gang members. It did not take long for her to rejoin the gang. This time around, she was much more involved. She started selling drugs and drinking. The only thing she hadn't done was murder anyone.

Riana became extremely out of control because there was no father figure around to bring balance in the household. After struggling in her schoolwork and not attending most of the time, she finally made the decision to drop out of school in the eleventh grade.

By the time it would have been her senior year, she had a juvenile record for drug possession and illegal use of a firearm. Stephanie was so stressed trying to look after her. In her mind, she wanted to kick Riana out of the house, but her heart wouldn't let her because of the love she developed for her over the years.

Riana spent several years on probation and in and out of the Juvenile Detention Center until she was seventeen. Her wrap sheet was so long that she couldn't get a legal job that paid minimum wage if she wanted. On her last charge, she was sentenced to three years in prison. The Upstate Women's Informatory was where she would serve her sentence.

Since her split with Frank, Stephanie had spent all those years alone without dating. Her friends made several attempts to send her out on blind dates, but she wasn't interested. Frank was her first love and she couldn't let him go.

Every year around Christmas time, Kimberly threw a

party for family and friends. This particular year the party was thrown at a fancy hotel ballroom. Stephanie didn't want to go because she normally went through a depression around the holidays every since her and Frank split. If she did not go Kimberly would literally come and drag her out of the house. While she was getting ready in the bathroom, Kimberly came storming through the bedroom door shouting.

"I know you better be ready or getting ready because if you're not I am going to dress and carry you out of this house myself."

Through the bathroom door, Stephanie replied, *"I am getting ready. Give me a minute."*

When Stephanie came out of the bathroom, Kimberly looked at her up and down and then said, *"Oh no! We have to do better than this."*

"What?"

Pointing down at her pants, she said, *"These! Jeans and a t-shirt? What do you think this is...a high school dance?"*

"This is not a t-shirt. It is a blouse. Besides, I love this shirt."

"No. No. No. I told you this was a formal event this year. Don't you have a nice dress that you can quickly slip on?"

"I don't have anything else to put on. All of my dresses

are old and too small. Besides, I don't feel sexy enough anymore to put on a dress."

"Nonsense. I had a feeling you were going to say something like that. This is why I took it upon myself to bring you one of my dresses."

"Girl...I'm not about put my behind in one of your dresses. That is so tacky and I don't know where your behind has been."

Replying with a little laugh, "With your daddy. Try on the dress so we can go. We're already late."

Stephanie tried on the dress and found that it fit very well. Looking at herself in the mirror, turning around, and sucking in her stomach, she felt very good.

"I must admit. I like this. I guess you have some taste after all."

"Whatever! Now, can we go please? The host is not supposed to be late."

Kimberly fixed Stephanie's hair and they headed out to the party. The color scheme of the party was white. The setting was so beautiful. All of the tables were covered with white tablecloths and white candles were burning everywhere. White lights were beautifully dimmed throughout the room. With all the white, it made the atmosphere really feel like Christmas.

While everyone was enjoying themselves by dancing and talking, Stephanie sat alone at her table. Several guys asked her to dance and made attempts to hold conversations with her, but she kept turning them away.

After Kimberly made her rounds speaking and thanking all of the guests, she went over to the table where Stephanie was sitting to talk to her.

"Why are you being such a dud?" asked Kimberly.

"I'm not. I just don't feel like dancing or talking."

"Come with me. I have a surprise for you."

Kimberly grabbed Stephanie's hand and led her out of the ballroom to the hotel bar area. When they got to the bar area, Kimberly went to go and get the surprise.

"Wait right here. I'll be back. Now, you can't look this way because if you do the surprise will be ruined," said Kimberly as she walked off.

When Kimberly walked away Stephanie wanted to turn around to see what the surprise was, but she didn't. After about five minutes of waiting, Stephanie was getting impatient and was about to turn around. Just before she did, Kimberly came back with the surprise.

"Ok. You can turn around now."

When Stephanie turned around her, heart started racing. She was in such shock that she couldn't get a word out of her mouth. Dressed in all white and looking sharp as a pack of razors, the surprise said, *"Merry Christmas. How are you?"*

With teary eyes she replied, *"I'm doing better as of*

now."

Kimberly wanted to give them some privacy. She gave both of them a hug and walked away.

"Would you like to sit and talk?"

"Yes. I would love to."

Like a gentleman, he pulled up a seat for the two of them and assisted her in sitting before he sat down.

"How has everything been?"

"Honestly, Frank. Not so good. Things just haven't been the same since you left. The house feels so empty with no one there but me."

"I really missed you. There has not been a day that I haven't thought about you."

"Same here. Are you dating anyone?"

"No. I'll be honest. I have been on a few dates, but that's about it. What about you?"

"I can't say the same. I never wanted to be with anyone but you, so it was hard for me to go out with another guy. I mean I loved you or shall I say love you so much that there is no one else I want. I can truly say you have my heart."

With a big smile on his face, he asked, *"Can I have my wife back?"*

"Here she is!"

At that moment, all of her pain and insecurities left. Love and security took its place.

When they finished talking, Frank led her back into the ballroom and they danced the night away. Her eyes were closed and her head lay peacefully against his chest. After the party, they went back to the house to talk. Stephanie had so much fun with him that she didn't want the night to end so they lay, hugged and…you figure out the rest.

Chapter 5

The Reunion

Several years have passed since I started my job. Steadily, I grew with the company. After only one year on the job, I was appointed the team leader of the financial department. This caused a few employees to envy me because of the length of time they had been with the company and weren't awarded the position.

Based on my income, I guess you could say I was getting a taste of the good life. Along with the good life, came the attitude. Everything about me changed. All of a sudden, I became this high class, stuck up person. They say money changes people. I was an example of that saying. My grandmother didn't raise me to be that way, but once you're grown, you start to make your own decisions. Folks down south would say, I was starting to smell myself.

One afternoon while heading out for lunch, I stopped at the ATM in the lobby to take out some cash. Entering the building was a guy that looked familiar to me. While passing each other, we made direct eye contact, but neither one of us spoke. The guy kept looking at me because he thought he had seen me somewhere before. Before I could walk out of the building, he rushed over and introduced himself.

"Hello. I'm Anthony. I couldn't help but to come over and speak to you. You look familiar. Where do I know you from?"

"We met a few years back at your father's club."

"You're absolutely right. Your name is Samantha...isn't it?"

"Yes. This is me."

"How have you been?"

"I'm fine. Just working hard trying to make it through everyday life. And yourself?"

"I have been ok, trying to do the same thing. It's all you can, do right?"

"Just about."

"I know you are probably in a rush and I have to get going, but I was wondering if I can leave you my number and we can catch up on some things?"

"Sure. That would be fine."

After writing down his number, he had to make a sarcastic comment before he walked off.

"You are going to call me like you did the last time...right? I really enjoyed talking to you."

I couldn't help but to smile and reply in a giggling voice.

"I will this time. Enjoy the rest of your evening."

"You do the same."

After talking to Anthony, I went to have lunch at the local diner a few blocks from my job. Over lunch, I was contemplating whether or not I should call him. The thought of him being a player kept surfacing through my mind because of the two different girls I saw him with. This was the reason why I hesitated to make the call.

For more than a week, I went back and forth with myself until I finally made the decision to call him.

"Hello."

"Hello. How are you?"

"Who am I speaking to?"

"Who do you think you are talking to?"

"I don't recognize the number, that's why I'm asking."

In a disguised voice, I pretended to be someone else.

"This is Stacy. What are you doing?"

"Oh, what's up? I thought you were someone playing on my phone. I was just thinking about you."

Before he could get too deep into the conversation and said something that would turn me off, I revealed myself.

"I'm joking. This is Samantha."

With a giggle he replied, *"You play too much. How are you?"*

"I'm doing fine. I see you are a very important man."

"It's not the way you think it is. I have a cousin named Stacy that I am close to. We speak on the regular. That's why I thought it could have been her."

In the back of my mind, all I could think of were the memories he last left me with. I answered in a sarcastic way.

"Oh, ok."

"I'm glad you called. I thought you were going to stand me up like the last time."

"Well, I didn't stand you up. I lost your number. I said I would call and I did."

"I really appreciate you keeping your word. Well, look...I'm still working right know. Can I give you a call back at this number?"

"Sure. This is my home phone. Talk to you later."

"Ok. Bye."

About two hours later he called me back. I was on my way to sleep, but stayed awake to talk to him. We talked for several hours. I knew I had to be to work in a few hours, but didn't care because I was really enjoying his conversation. Being on the phone that time of night brought me back to my younger days. With all the blushing and smiling, I was doing on the phone, I began to feel like a little shy schoolgirl. Night after night, the more we talked, the later I found myself going to bed. He had a way of making a girl lose focus.

After a week, we went on a movie and dinner date. There was not one second during the entire night that I wasn't smiling. At this time in my life, I had never been with a guy that made me feel the way he did. He was tall, dark, intelligent, well dressed and had a wonderful personality. Needles to say, I was falling fast.

Like most women, I was forcing myself to think that there was nothing there, but on the inside, I knew he had tapped into my heart.

To top the night off, he took me to an old southern style blues club. It was a small club, but it was full of entertainment. The dance floor was a decent size for a small joint. On this particular night, a live band was playing. On the last song of the night, Anthony had requested a slow song. He then grabbed me by the hand and led me to the dance floor. Despite not having any rhythm, I did not want to spoil the flow of the night, so I followed his lead. With all of the people dancing around us, I felt at one with him, like there was no one else but the band and us and they were singing for us. With my eyes shut and head rested softly on his chest, it felt like I was floating on a cloud.

When we left the club, I was tired and ready to go

home. My feet were hurting from the sexy heels I desperately wanted to wear for Anthony. I guess beauty really is pain.

This time when he drove me home, I wanted him to walk me to the door. When we got up to the door, I took my keys out and started dangling them as if I couldn't find the right key to open the door. I was trying to give him a sign that I didn't really want him to leave. Immediately he asked, *"Can I come in?"*

"I don't know if that would be a good idea."

"I'm sorry, but I just had a wonderful time with you tonight and don't want it to end."

Before I could answer, he aggressively grabbed me by the waist and pulled me towards him and we started kissing. That was all it took. I was too afraid to make the first move because I was worried about him putting a label on me.

When we finally got in the house, there was nonstop kissing that lead to him spending the night and leaving me with backaches. From this point on, we saw each other everyday and became close. Well, at least that was what I thought.

Chapter 6

The Truth

After more than five trips down to Georgia, the Lovinskis finally found a new home that fit their standards. The house sat in a gated community located just ten minutes south of Savannah. There were a lot of children in the neighborhood that Briana could make friends with. The scenery was the total opposite of New Jersey. Adapting to a slower lifestyle would take some getting use to, but they all were up to the challenge.

Three months later, Danielle opened the new office. The employment inquiries were filling up fast due to her reputation up north. Before long, she had a fully operative office. Susan wanted to be a stay-at-home mom, but in order to maintain their lifestyle; she knew she had to go back to work. At first, she went to work for a local real estate brokerage until she made her name reputable. Then, she started her own brokerage.

It didn't take long before Briana made a few friends. Her new best friend was named Veronica. They connected right away. Veronica was also adopted, but lived with a straight, African American couple. Her mother was on drugs and she never knew her father. After going from house to house, she finally found a place she could call home.

Now, that graduation was a few days away. She hadn't decided whether she wanted to go to college or become a licensed real estate broker and work for Susan.

One evening, while coming in from Veronica's house, she overheard Susan talking to Danielle in the kitchen. There was a swinging door that separated the dining room from the kitchen, so Briana hid behind the door and listened.

"Ms. Anderson called today," said Susan.

"What did she say?"

"She was calling to do a regular check up on Briana. For some reason her twin sister crossed my mind so I asked about her. She said that she has been in and out of trouble for some time now and is currently serving a prison sentence."

"Did she tell you the reason?"

"No. We didn't get that far into the conversation because she had to leave. It's funny that her sister had been on my mind and Ms. Anderson called and informed me of her situation. I have been wanting to tell..."

Before she could finish, Briana ran upstairs to her room and locked the door. Her first instinct was to go back down stairs and confront them both for not telling her, but instead she stayed in her room and cried because she felt betrayed.

For the next few days, she kept to herself. She didn't want to talk to either one of her parents. Susan saw there was something wrong with her, but didn't ask because she knew eventually she would come to her to talk about the problem that was troubling her.

After gradation Briana and Veronica's family went out to dinner to celebrate together. As soon as they got home, Briana called both Susan and Danielle in the kitchen to talk. Susan always led the conversations.

"I noticed the way you have been moping around here like something is bothering you. What is on your mind?"

To make sure she did not come off disrespectful, she took a deep breath and answered.

"The other night, when I came into the house, I overheard you two in here saying that I have a twin sister. How could you keep something like that from me for all of these years? Don't you think that was important for me to know?

I love you two very much, but it is just as important for me to know my blood relatives."

"We are very sorry. I have wanted to tell you that for some time now but never got around to doing so. We wanted you to get comfortable with us before we told you certain things. It's not like we were keeping it from you because we didn't want you to know your real family members. Look at us. We are White Americans and you are African American, so we knew there were questions we had to answer one day, but since you never asked, telling you slipped my mind."

"This news has got me lost to the point that I don't know if I want to know now or not. I'm going to take a shower and lay down. I have a headache. I will see you both in the morning."

For the next week, she stayed locked in her room. Susan and Danielle felt so bad that they took it upon themselves to do some research to find her sisters. Danielle called in a favor to one of her old friends back in New Jersey, a private investigator, to locate Riana and I.

A week later, he faxed the findings to Danielle's office. As soon as she got home that day she handed them to Susan. Briana was upstairs in her room sleeping. With a soft knock on the door Susan asked, *"Can I come in?"*

"Yes," answered Briana.

She came in and sat on the edge of the bed to talk to

her.

"I know you don't want to be bothered, so I won't stay. I just came up here to drop something off to you. I think this is something you will be interested in. It will help answer some of the questions you might have. I'm going to leave it here on the dresser for you. You take a look at it when you are ready."

Susan then kissed her on the forehead and left the room. Briana was curious to know what was in the envelope, but didn't get up right away to see. For several hours, she tossed and turned trying to fall asleep, but she couldn't because of her curiosity. Finally, she got up and turned on the lamp to see what was in the envelope. When she opened it, the answers to all of her questions, and more, were in there. Susan had also included a roundtrip airline voucher in the envelope so she could take a flight up to New Jersey and meet them. She stayed up all night filling out the visitation forms, writing letters and staring at the picture of her splitting image. The thought of someone who looked just like her couldn't sink in, until she got to actually see it for herself. There was no picture of me, only an address of where I lived. She didn't include her home phone number in either letter because she wanted to break the ice through mail to see if we would write back. If we wrote her back, it would mean a lot to her because it would show that we were interested in getting to know her.

The next morning when she awoke, the first thing she did was go outside to drop the letters in the mail. It took a week to reach Riana because of the security procedures at the prison. When she received the letter, her first thought was not to open it because no one had ever wrote her before and she didn't recognize the name. She sat it next to her bed. For three days the letter sat there until her curiosity got the best of her. Fifteen minutes before lockdown, she picked it up and started reading. The letter read

Dear Riana,

How are you? I must first start off by saying this is the most confusing letter I have ever written. My name is Briana. Since birth, I have lived with my adopted parents. I never knew anything about my real family members until recently. I am writing you for this reason. I know this is going to be hard for you to believe, but we are twin sisters. This is why our names are similar. Our mother died after she gave birth to you and I. Her name was Juanita. We also have an older sister by the name of Samantha. Our now deceased grandmother raised her. This is all fresh news to me also. I found out about a week ago. I would love to get to know you and catch up on all the lost time if this is okay with you.

I am looking forward to hearing from you.

Your Sister,
Briana

Riana did not know what to think at first. She also didn't know the reason why she was adopted because her adopted parents never told her. Riana thought that if this were so, Stephanie would have told her a long time ago. The only reason she wrote back was to let Briana know she had the wrong person. Riana's letter read.

Dear Briana,

Your story seemed very interesting but unfortunately I think you have me confused with another Riana. Our names and stories are similar, but if I had a sister I would have known by now. I thank you for the letter anyways. Hope you find who you are looking for.

Sorry,
Riana

Around the same time, I received her letter in mail. All day at work I had a gut feeling that something was going to happen but didn't know what it was. When I got home from work, I checked the mailbox. Flipping through the mail, I froze when I saw the envelope from Briana. The rush that went through my body was greater than that of a skydiver. Even winning the lottery couldn't give me this amount of joy. The best thing I can say is that this moment was priceless.

After shedding many tears of joy, I immediately grabbed a pen and paper and wrote Briana a letter. My letter read.

Dear Little Sis,

This has been a long time coming. I am going to start this letter off by introducing myself because you were too young to remember me. My name is Samantha. I remember the last day I saw you before your adopting parents took you and your twin sister away. If you didn't know, you have a twin. I was eight at that time and it had to be one of the saddest moments of my short life. For many years, there has been a void in my heart and now it is half complete. I never thought I would get this chance to talk you. Our grandmother always said that God works in mysterious ways. Today, I am a believer. I can't wait until I can hear your voice, see your face and give you the biggest kiss and hug I can find. I can go on with this letter for days because there is so much we have to catch up on, but I won't. The address you have for me is my old address from college. My new address is on the envelope. My home number is (635) 735-2607. Feel free to call me anytime. Take care of yourself and call me as soon as you can.

Love Always,
Samantha

I was so excited that I called Aunt Stacy to share the news. Aunt Stacy was excited as well because thoughts of the twins often crossed her mind.

Two weeks from the date the letters were mailed to Riana and I, Briana received reply letters from us both. The first letter she opened was from Riana. Reading the letter made her a little disappointed because those were not the words she wanted to hear. In her mind, she had already prepared herself for any outcome. This is why she didn't get too upset. A hesitation to open my letter came over her. She was afraid of getting the same results, but she opened it anyway. The words quickly jumped out of the letter and she immediately began to feel better. The highlight of the letter was the phone number I gave her.

Briana was nervous and anxious about calling me. Before calling that evening she wrote Riana another letter.

This time she included a picture from her senior photos. After dinner, she went up to her room to call me. When she reached me, we talked for hours. We were so comfortable talking to each other that we felt like they had known each other for years. The connection was instant…the way a sister relationship should be. From that day forth, we spoke at least three times a week.

A week later, Riana received a second letter. Once more, she let it sit next to her bed for a couple of days. Yet again, curiosity got the best of her. After reading the letter, she felt irritated because she had already told Briana that she had mistaken her for someone else. Just before throwing the letter in the trash, she felt something remaining in the envelope. When she pulled it out, the walls of her tough guy mentality came crashing down. For the first time in many years, she felt helpless. Looking at the picture, both confused her and freaked her out. It was like someone had sent a picture of herself. Despite being a tomboy, she saw a feminine side to what she could look like.

That night, Riana sat up all night thinking to herself. A lot of thoughts were running through her head. She was trying to figure out why Stephanie never told her and how do she go about getting to know a stranger, who is her twin sister.

The next morning, right at the crack of dawn, she wrote her sister again. This time, the letter was the opposite of the last one.

Dear Briana,

How are you? First, let me start off by saying I'm sorry. I know you were just as shocked to find out as I am, so you should understand why I responded to your initial letter the way I did. When I received your second letter I almost didn't read it. Something told me to open it. When I read it and looked at the picture, it freaked me out to see someone who looked the same as I do. I would like to keep communication and see you someday. I hope you accept my apology.

Your sister,
Riana

After communicating with her sisters for a month, Riana used her flight voucher and came to see us. When she landed at the airport, I was already excitedly awaiting her arrival near the baggage claim. As soon as Riana got off the plane, she phoned me to ask my location. When we spotted each other, we immediately ran towards each other, embraced, and cried tears of joy.

Since Riana was going to be in town for a week, I had a lot of activities planned for them. That afternoon, we had an appointment at the spa. Later on that evening, we drove down to our grandmother's old house, which was passed down to Aunt Stacy, for a long awaited surprise party. The house was decorated with flowers and balloons throughout. When she walked through the door, each family member greeted her with a gift. The love she received was so overwhelming that again she began to cry. After meeting everyone and receiving all her gifts, Briana was ready to have her first encounter with some good old southern cooking prepared by Aunt Stacy, that has been passed down for generations. After dinner they all sat around, talked, and had a few drinks...nonalcoholic beverages for the miners of course. The best thing about this gathering was that there was not any arguing or fighting between the adults or children.

It was one of those moments in life when one wished they could freeze time. All the money in the world couldn't pay for it. The best way to describe that moment was priceless. Family times are supposed to be filled with fun and laughter. Instead we focus our energy on what is best for me, rather than us. We also spend too much time complaining and whining about what the family doesn't do, rather than trying to resolve the issue by discussing the problem. If you don't talk about it, how can someone else know about it? Communication is key. **We have to do better.**

The day had been long and exhausting for Briana, so we headed back to my place so she could get some rest.

The next morning, I woke up early and made Briana breakfast in bed.

I'm talking about some homemade butter biscuits, eggs, bacon, sausage and a bowl of hot grits with a slice of melted cheese on top. If that wasn't enough, she had an ice cold, almost frozen glass of orange juice. After eating a meal like this, she caught the disease that most people get after eating a large meal and wanted to go back to sleep, but couldn't because we had a schedule to keep.

Later that morning, we got dressed and drove two hours west to visit Riana. Since this was our first time meeting her and visiting a prison, we felt as if we were walking the Green Mile themselves.

Being that this was a state penitentiary, contact visits were allowed. Before entering the visiting room, they had to go through a security check. The search was so thorough that they felt like the criminals. Even though the visitation was called contact visits, we were only allowed a hug and kiss before and after visits. As soon as we entered the room, Riana spotted Briana. Of course, it wasn't hard spotting her mirror image. When she approached us, we held hands, cried, and hugged with our hearts. Within the short hour of visitation, so much was discussed. The whole time was spent joking and laughing. From the outside looking in, you would think the three of us were very close. At the end of the visit, we held hands again and said, " I love you" to each other. This time there wasn't any tear shedding because we knew we would see each other again, soon.

Usually, it is hard to have an open conversation when you reunite or first meet someone, mainly because our past experiences have taught us that time has a way of changing people. Eventually, their true colors will surface. It's very rare to meet someone and make an immediate connection. When this happens, hold on because great people don't come in our lives too often. With a sincere person, you don't have to look for their colors because they love to expose them for everyone to see.

A week had passed and now it was time for Briana to go back home. She took forever to get ready, because she didn't want to leave. When I dropped her off at the airport, she missed her flight. I had to return to work the next morning and Briana had to get back home to register for school, so she was put on stand by and caught a later flight. I waited with her for two hours, but had to leave. Before I left, Briana had pretended to go to the restroom, but really went to the gift shop to get me a thank you card. After we hugged and shed more tears, Briana gave me the card and told me not to open it until I got home.

As soon as I got to her car, I opened the letter. My curiosity wouldn't let me wait until I got home. The card read:

Big Sis,

First, let me start off by thanking God for bringing you into my life. Then, I would like to thank you for being the person you are. Every morning, I wake up and think how blessed I am to have a big sister like you. This past week has been, by far, the best time in my life. Every second with you was a memorable moment. I know the future has more great times in store for us to share. I can't wait until we can do this again.

Love Always,
Briana

The card was so heartfelt that I put it in my collection of memories. You know, the one we all have, where we usually keep some of our old letters or cards from a previous relationship or even movie ticket stubs. Every now and then, you pull them out and reminisce on those moments and say, " *Those were the good old days*".

Over the next year and a half, the three of us became really close. My career and relationship with Anthony were both doing well. Briana was doing good in school and Riana is taking classes to get her G.E.D. Every two and a half to three months, Briana would fly up and visit. Our time together was greatly valued. The only thing we were missing was Riana. This didn't last much longer. She was sentenced to three years of incarceration, but was released early due to good behavior. On the day of Riana's release, Briana flew up to be here when the gates to our sister's freedom opened once again.

Briana and I were parked along the dirt road. From afar, we could see the officers escorting her through the gates. For security reasons, there were several gates they had to go through before they got to the gate that exited the grounds. At 5:15 p.m., Riana was finally freed. When the last gate was closed, it closed a chapter in Riana's life, but opened a lifetime for the three of us.

For at least ten minutes, we stood outside hugging each other with our eyes closed. Closing your eyes, whether kissing or hugging meant that you were really into that moment.

Riana came out with the same clothing she had on when she initially got arrested. Briana and I took her shopping to buy a new outfit and a pair of shoes. Since she was never the feminine type, everything she picked out was boyish. We wanted to encourage her to pick something more girly, but didn't because we were just happy to see her.

After the shopping we went back to my place to get ready for a night out on the town. Since this was Riana's first time here, I gave her a tour and showed her some of my memorable photos.

Previously, reservations were made at a fine dining restaurant. I wanted Riana to see the other side of life. Walking into the restaurant, Riana felt out of place because the atmosphere felt a little uppity. The only places she had ever eaten at were fast food restaurants and soul food diners. A lot of the words on the menu she couldn't even pronounce, so she let me order for her. When the food was served, it didn't look too appealing to Riana, but when she tasted it all of her preconceived notions went out the door.

We talked and laughed while having dinner. Briana was the most expressive one. She felt the need to express her feelings for them.

"This is more than a dream come true. There is nothing more I could ask for, besides our mother being here with us. I am so happy being around you two. It really bothers me to know that I only get to see you both for a few days, then I have to leave again."

"Why don't you move up here?" asked Riana.

"I would love to, but it would be too exhausting trying to go to school fulltime, work a fulltime job and shuffle the bills that come along with having your own place."

Without hesitation, I replied, *"You can stay with me. I would love for you to. Besides, we still have a whole lot to catch up on. What do you say?"*

"I can't just say yes right now. I have to give it some

thought. What school will I attend?"

"Let me handle that part. All I need is for you to say yes."

"I'm seriously going to think about it and let you know my decision."

The next morning, Riana and I took Briana to the airport because she had school the following day. During the course of her flight, she thought deeply to herself about what would truly make her happy. At first, she was going back and forth with why she should and shouldn't move to New Jersey. She loved Danielle and Susan because they took very good care of her. They were the only parents she had ever known, but her heart was with her sisters. On that flight, she made her final decision to move and be with them. The only problem she had now was figuring out the easiest way break the news to her parents without hurting them.

When she got off the plane, Danielle and Susan were waiting for her at baggage claim. From a distance, Susan could see there was something wrong from Briana's facial expressions, so it changed her approach. Instead of a happy voice, she switched to a more concerned tone and asked, *"How was your trip?"*

"It was fine."

She thought Briana would share her weekend. Particularly about her sister's release from prison, but she didn't.

Seeing that her answer was short, Susan didn't bother to ask her any more questions. Instead, she ended the conversation by saying, *"Okay. Well, the car is this way."*

When they reached home, Briana went directly to her room. From then until dinner, she had several hours to practice how she was going to tell them. Family discussions usually took place over dinner. On her way down stairs, her palms were sweating profusely. When she sat down, she immediately began to eat without waiting for her parents. Seeing this, Susan stopped her and questioned her behavior.

"Tell me what is bothering you. I noticed something was wrong with you at the airport but I didn't say anything because I thought you would talk about it when you were ready. You used to come and talk to me when you had a problem, but now I have to force it out of you. Do you not feel comfortable talking to me anymore?"

"It's not that...I do. It's just I don't know how to tell you certain things without hurting you."

"Don't you think it would hurt us more if you didn't tell us and we found out from someone else?" asked Danielle.

"Yes. I tell you everything. It may take me a little while because I try to wait for the right time."

"Okay. We're listening."

After a long pause, she began telling them.

"How do I say this? Well, after talking to my sisters we all feel there is so much to catch up on. I really want to get

to know them better. In order for that to happen, I will have to move to New Jersey."

"Are you asking or telling us you are moving to New Jersey?" asked Susan.

"I am almost twenty. I can make some decisions for myself, but I still wanted to know how you would feel about it before I make a decision of such magnitude."

"It sounds like you have already made up your mind," stated Danielle in an angry tone.

"Well, you are of legal age and able to make your own decisions, but from a parental view there are too many unknowns. I mean, you don't know how responsible they are, whether they make good decisions and most importantly, where are you going to live? I think you should stay here at least until you finish school because all of your credits may not be transferable and you will have to repeat those classes. If you remain here, you can focus directly on school because we are here to support you financially until you graduate. Then, if you still want to move you can find work there and be independent," said Susan in a calm tone.

"I understand your concern and all, but I think I really want to make this move. Samantha has a three-bedroom house and she wants me to come live with her. I don't want you to think that if I move up there I am going to forget about you. You are my parents. Biological or not, I still love you because you have always been there for me. I

don't want to beat around the bush...my desire is to move and be with them."

Before walking out of the room in tears, Susan replied, *"If that's what you wish...fine."*

That night, for the first time since Briana was old enough to feed herself, they didn't eat dinner together. For more than a week, there were little words spoken to each other. Susan was hurt and the only way she knew how to deal with it was to stay to herself.

Over the next few weeks, Briana would do everything she needed to do in order to make the move. I had an old friend register Briana in classes for her for the next semester. The only thing left for her to do was pack and make the trip.

It took some time for Susan to accept that Briana was leaving. Eventually, she got it. On the day of her departure, both of her parents were there to see her off. They hugged and cried after Susan gave her some words of encouragement. To help her out, they gave her an inspirational card and a check for one thousand dollars. Briana was so happy to see that they supported her decision. She wished she could have met her biological mother, but not in a million years would she have traded the life she knew with Danielle and Susan. It was one of those once in a lifetime experiences. Now, she could begin another chapter of her life.

Chapter 7

The Make Up

During the time of Riana's incarceration, Stephanie only came to see her twice. It was a mutual agreement because it hurt her to see her daughter locked up behind bars like an animal. Riana didn't want to see her either because it made her upset when Stephanie had to leave. Not seeing her, or anyone else, made the time much easier to handle. When she was released, she knew there was no place to go, but back home. Because of all the trouble she kept getting herself into and the lack of respect she had for the household, Stephanie put her out. She had to ask for permission to come back home to stay.

On the following day of her release, I dropped Riana off at her old house. When she pulled up, Frank was taking the trash to the garbage bin on the side of the house. Before he could make it around the corner, Riana bumped into him and scared him. He quickly jumped back with his hand in defense mode. With his thumb and index finger an inch apart he said,

"Oh…man…you were this close to getting knocked out."

"Sorry."

"When did you get out?"

"Yesterday. When did you come back home?"

"I've been back for a while. What brings you around here?"

" Well, I stopped by to say hello and to see if I can stay here for a few nights until I find somewhere to live."

"That's not up to me. You have to ask Stephanie. She's sleeping, but you can go in and ask her."

"Never mind. I'll find somewhere else to sleep tonight."

Before she turned around to walk away, he grabbed her by the arm and said, *"Wait a minute. You can stay here to-night. I rather know that you are here and safe than to worry about you."*

"What about Stephanie?"

"Don't worry about that. I can handle her. Who is the person that dropped you off?"

"Long story."

He then, grabbed her by the hand and walked her into

the house.

Driving away, I felt really bad that I didn't offer to let Riana stay at my house until she got on her feet but I didn't know if I could trust her yet.

Hearing the beep from the alarm system when the door opened, woke Stephanie up. Rolling over and not feeling Frank laying next to her made her get out of bed to see where he was. When she walked out of the room, Riana was walking up the stairs.

"Oh my God! He really does answer prayers. I was just praying for you to come home. How are you sweetie?" asked Stephanie in surprise, with both hands over her mouth.

"I'm fine."

"Come down and give me a hug. I guess you need somewhere to stay."

"Yes, ma'am."

"You can come back home on three accounts. You find a job; no more gang involvement and you come to church on Sundays. Fair enough?"

"Agreed."

Stephanie did not care that she had to be at work early in the morning. She was so happy to see Riana that the three of them stayed up most of the night talking and looking through old family pictures. Riana told them about how we reunited. Stephanie apologized for not telling her, but she had already forgiven her. Finally, around 5 a.m., they all fell asleep in the family room on the couch.

Stephanie had to be up for work a few hours later, but she was too tired to go in. She wanted to spend the day with Riana, so she put on her sick voice and called out from work. Later on that morning, they got up and got dressed for a day out together. First, they went for breakfast at a black-owned restaurant that served southern style meals. Then, they went to the mall to buy Riana some clothes and personal items. When they got back to the house, Riana wanted to go for a walk. On her journey around the neighborhood, she decided to stop by and say what's up to her set brothers.

Looking from inside the house where they sold their drugs, Lil Jay saw her and came out to talk.

"Hey, what's up? When did you get out?"

"I got out a couple of days ago."

"You ready to go back to work?"

"No. I'll pass."

"I never got a chance to thank you for taking those bullets for me, so thank you."

The reason Riana went to prison on her last charge was because of Lil Jay. One evening all of the gang members were hanging on the block when the DEA came out of nowhere to do a street sweep. Riana didn't have any drugs on her at the time so she knew she was okay. Lil Jay saw them coming and quickly threw his sack of drugs. He knew he was on his last strike. With guns drawn, the officers ordered everyone to get on their knees with their hands behind their heads. Two of the cops were doing the body searches while the others still had their guns drawn. When they got to Riana and Lil Jay, one of the cops found the sack next to Riana. She wanted to say it wasn't hers, but loyalty and fear got in the way. Looking Lil Jay in the eyes, he gave her a look as if he was saying she better not say anything, so she kept her mouth shut. They arrested her and took her away for the next two and a half years for something she didn't do. This is one of those incidents where you take the word loyal out of loyalty and replace it with stupid.

Pulling out a roll of money from his pocket, he said, *"Here, take this. It's a little something to show my appreciation and to help you get back on your feet 'till you come back home."*

When he gave her the money, he went back into the house. As he was walking away, a black SUV pulled up. The front seat passenger got out, went to the back, and pulled out a black brief case. Two of the other men with him escorted him into the house.

In Riana's mind, she was thinking that the guy must have been dropping off drugs rather than money because Lil Jay wasn't a major supplier. All of his money came in moderation from all of his petty dealers.

She wanted to know what was going on. She asked her set brother, Mookie.

"Who is that?"

"That's the new supplier."

"What happened to Rico?"

"You know how it was with Rico. He thought he could keep shorting us and nothing was gonna be said, so him and Lil Jay had an exchange of words that escalated into something serious and now he ain't around no more."

Mookie was the shady type who couldn't be trusted as far as you could throw him, and he was a big boy. Lil Jay only kept him around because he was willing to do whatever at any given time.

On their way back to the car, the guy holding the brief case looked Riana up and down. Then, puckered his lips as if he was giving her a kiss and smirked, but didn't say anything. His face had looked familiar to her, but she couldn't remember where she saw him before. After that she went back home before someone saw her over there and the word got back to Stephanie. She remembered her promise to stay away.

Chapter 8
The Calamity

Ever since Briana moved up to be with us sisters, we made a promise to see each other at least three times a week. One of the days was dedicated to a ladies night out…even if it was going out for dinner, clubbing, or both.

One night, we decided to go out for dinner only. The temperature was just right, so we decided to eat outside. While ordering, Anthony called me to see what my plans were for the night.

"Hey baby. What are you doing?"

"I'm out having dinner with my sisters."

In a disappointed tone he replied, *"Oh. Well, I guess I'll talk to you later."*

"What's wrong?"

"Nothing. I just wanted to know if you wanted to get something to eat with me tonight since we haven't spent much time together lately, but it's okay."

"You can come have dinner with us. I'm sure they won't mind. Besides, I want you all to meet each other. We're downtown. Where are you?"

"I'm not that far away. I'll stop by and meet them. See you in a minute. Bye."

I told them that Anthony was stopping by to meet them and would probably have dinner also and they got excited. They were anxious to meet the guy who was responsible for making me so happy.

Several minutes later, Anthony pulled up in his Mercedes-Benz. At that time, Riana was out front smoking a cigarette. As soon as he got out, this feeling of nervousness came over her. All of a sudden, the pieces of the puzzle came together. The guy who she saw at the drug house looked familiar because he was the same guy on the pictures at my house.

When Anthony came over to the table, I got up and gave him a kiss and hug. Then, I turned towards my sisters and introduced him to them. Briana stood up and shook his hand, but Riana didn't budge. She just waved and looked the other way. At that moment, he too remembered seeing her at the drop and thought, *"Oh boy"* to himself.

Briana and Anthony conversed with each other the entire night at dinner while Riana sat quietly. I noticed the change in her attitude, but did not say anything because I didn't want to spoil the evening, in case an argument would have started.

During the course of the ride home, Riana still wasn't saying anything. She wanted to tell me about Anthony, but didn't because she was afraid of hurting me. She could not fall asleep until she got it off of her mind. The only way to do that was to tell. About 3:30 in the morning, she got up and called me. Hearing the phone ring, I answered quickly.

"Hello."

"Sorry, to wake you, but there is something I need to talk to you about."

"I'm listening."

"I know you noticed a change in my attitude tonight. The reason is because of Anthony."

I quickly got up and left the room because he was lying next to me.

"What about him?"

"The day after I got out of prison, I went through the neighborhood to say hello to some old friends when this black SUV pulled up. Three guys got out, but one of them was carrying a black brief case. I was wondering

what they were doing there, so I asked my set brother. He told me that they were the new suppliers for their drug operation. On their way out, I got a good look at the guy carrying the brief case because he looked at me and blew a kiss my way. I knew he had looked familiar, but I couldn't figure out where I had seen him before. Tonight, when I saw Anthony, it came to me that he was the one on the pictures at your house and the guy dropping off the drugs. I wanted to say something then, but I knew it wasn't the right time."

"Are you sure it was Anthony? He doesn't drive a black SUV. I have seen all of his cars and an SUV is not one of them."

"I'm telling you, it was him. I got a good look at him when he looked me in the face. I don't know who the SUV belonged to, but it was him carrying that black brief case."

"Are you positive about this?"

"Yes. I wouldn't make something up like this. I know how you feel about him that's why it was hard for me to tell you this."

After hanging up the phone I went back into the bedroom. I wanted to wake him up and ask him about it, but my love was getting in the way.

Sometimes when people are so wrapped up in relationships, they tend to become blind to the things around them out of fear of losing that person. They ignore certain signs or information given to them, as in cases like this. You cannot believe everything you hear but it doesn't hurt to ask questions or look into matters. People are not mind readers, so if you don't ask you will never find the answer you are looking for, but be careful. You might find out more than you wanted to know.

A couple of weeks had gone by and I still had not said anything to Anthony about Riana's accusations. It wouldn't be until one evening when Anthony came over and asked why I had been acting so differently lately. My conscience would not allow me to hold it in any longer. I told him why.

"Why have you been lying to me?"

"About what?"

"I told you how I felt about drug dealers. My father died because of that lifestyle and then you go and do the same thing. You told me you worked for your father, but you forgot to add in this part of your life. What is it that you really do?"

"First of all, I don't have to answer to you. Secondly, you just met her. How are you going to believe her over me?"

"I never said there was a her. It must be true."

"I don't know what you are talking about or who

you got your information from, but they got the wrong person."

"Look, I don't want to argue or fight but I need some time to myself to think. I think it would be best if we not see each other for a while so until I can figure this out."

In an aggressive tone, he replied, *"It's not over until I say it's over."*

Heading towards the door to let him out, I said, *"I think you need to leave."*

He got upset and grabbed me by the arm with a tight grip. I didn't like anyone grabbing me. I snatched my arm away from him and mistakenly hit him in the face. In return, he slapped me across the face and punched me in the arm knocking me to the ground. I then burst into tears and threatened to call the police, so he quickly left.

That night, he kept calling my phone, but I wouldn't answer. I told her sisters what happened and they got upset. Riana felt like some of it was her fault and wanted to get even with him for hitting her. He was afraid to come by the house because he knew I would call the police, so he just followed me around.

Two weeks later, he finally caught up with me on our girls' night out at a bar. I spotted him coming our way and alerted my sisters that we had to leave immediately. We made it out of the building, but he caught up to us before we could make it to the car. Grabbing me by the arm, he said, *"I need to talk to you."*

Jerking my arm away from him, I replied, *"There is nothing to talk about. Let go of my arm."*

Riana got upset and started pulling on my arm to help free it. He didn't like her because he felt none of this would have happened if she didn't tell. He told her to mind her own business and to step away from him. She then grabbed his arm with both hands and tried to pull him away from me. He got more upset and then hit her across the face. Grabbing her lip and seeing blood on her finger, she got furious and said, *"You messed up now. You better watch your back because I got something for you."*

Walking to their car, a group of guys saw Anthony hit Riana and ran over to help her. Seeing the guys come at him, Anthony immediately backed off and left.

When I dropped Riana off home, she went to the neighborhood to find her set brother, Trigger. The name should speak for itself. Every time there was a shoot out or a hit ordered, Trigger was the guy to take the shot. He was the one who introduced Riana to the gang life and had been friends with her ever since.

Trigger got real upset when he saw her face and wanted to go after Anthony. The only problem was that

Lil Jay probably wouldn't have approved the hit. They went ahead and did it on their own.

Trigger knew that Anthony hung out at one of his father's spots most of the time. Riding around for more than a two hours, they finally caught up with him at his father's bar. Trigger sent another set brother inside to scope out the place. When he went inside, Anthony was at the bar drinking. He waited around until Anthony got ready to leave and informed Trigger by phone. Anthony had several drinks, so he wasn't as alert as he should have been. Before he could get in his car, Trigger came up with Riana behind him and his 9mm drawn and ordered him to turn around. Trigger was a heartless person. He liked his victims to see his face before he murdered them.

"You like hitting women? Well, you hit the wrong one this time," said Trigger as he cocked his gun.

Anthony laughed and responded fearlessly.

"You have no idea who you're dealing with. Forget the both of you."

As soon as he said those words, two shots rang out, hitting him in the center mass of his chest. Riana stood in shock for a minute because she had never witnessed anyone murdered at close range. Trigger pulled her by the arm shoved her in the car.

Hearing the gunshots from inside, witnesses came

outside to see what was going on. When they saw Anthony lying on the ground and bleeding, they immediately called the paramedics. By the time they got to the scene, it was too late. Anthony had bled to death.

While sleeping at home, Mr. B. received a phone call that his son had been murdered. Immediately, he got up and called Orvy and his crew to meet him at the crime scene. When he got there the police had the area blocked off with the yellow "Do Not Cross" tape. One of the officers let him inside to I.D. the body. The paramedics pulled back the white sheet from Anthony's face and he confirmed that it was his son.

His first thought was revenge. After seeing the body, he went inside the bar to view the video recording of the parking lot. He didn't inform the police of the tape because he wanted to take matters into his own hands.

That morning during their daily meeting, Mr. B. ordered his guys to go through every neighborhood that was gang-related and ask questions and if they had to…use force by all means necessary until they found the answers they were looking for. If the person was found, he didn't want his guys to get rid of him because he wanted to be there.

After shaking down a few neighborhoods, their last stop was the 21st street gang. Pulling the car up closely to the curb with a gun pointed out the window, Orvy ordered one of the gangsters to get in the car. This one happened to be Mookie. Mookie, aka "The Word Man" was like a news broadcaster. Everything that went on in the streets, he knew about it. When questioned about Anthony, he pretended not to know anything until one of the gunmen wrapped his arms around his neck in a choking position. Still claiming he did not know anything, Orvy pointed a gun at him and told him to start talking or he was going to shoot him. Mookie could not breathe and felt like he was going to pass out, so he began to talk.

"Okay. I'll tell you what I know. Your guy was murdered by one of the brothers and sisters in my set."

"What are the their names?"

"The one who actually fired the shot is Brad, but known by everyone as Trigger. The girl is Frank's daughter. Her name is Riana."

"Why did they kill him?"

"I heard that your guy had hit her sister and when she tried to stop him, he hit her and she got upset and went to tell Trigger. The both of them have been friends for a long time, so Trigger got mad once she told him and he wanted to get even. Lil Jay didn't know anything about the hit until after it was done. If he did, he would have stopped it."

Mookie then told them where to find Trigger and

Riana. After kicking him out of the car, Orvy and the crew went back to the bar to tell Mr. B. the information that was attained. He didn't want to waste any time, so they headed back out to find Trigger. Finding him at the location that was given, the crew tortured and killed him.

Their next stop was Frank's house. When they got there, Frank was just pulling in the driveway, coming from work. Frank thought they were there to bribe him again. Walking towards the front door, he said, *"I told you before and I'll tell you again...I'm not interested."*

Mr. B. instantly got furious over Frank's attitude.

"This is not about that. What I'm here about is on a whole different level," said Mr. B., as he slammed the car door.

Frank saw how mad he was and did not want to push his luck.

"Where is your daughter?" asked Mr. B as he walked towards Frank.

"Why are you asking?"

"I hear she has something to do with the murder of my son and I want to talk to her."

"I haven't seen her in days so I can't help you."

"Frank, unless you want my son's blood on your hands, I suggest you start talking before you and your family end up with him."

"I said I didn't..."

Before he could finish what he was going to say, Orvy pulled his gun out and pointed it at Frank's head. This was when Frank realized how serious the situation was. Knowing the capabilities of Mr. B., he didn't want to become victim of his rage, so he told him everything he wanted to know.

The guys then piled back into the cars and headed to my house. Frank felt like a coward now that he betrayed his daughter. Parents are supposed to protect their kids from harm, no matter what it takes...even if it involved risking their own lives.

Frank waited until they turned the corner leaving his house, then tried to call Riana several times to inform her of the situation, but she never answered. After several attempts of calling and not getting through, he ran in the house as fast as he could to get his gun and then ran back out and jumped in his truck to follow the guys to my house.

When the guys got to my house, they kicked in the front door with their guns drawn just in case someone was inside. Searching the house, Mr. B. saw Anthony's photos all over the house and became confused. He didn't know what to think, but there was something strange going on.

Parked on the next block, Frank sat in his truck and

observed what was going on. His plan was to tail the guys just in case they found Riana before he did, so he could alert her. A few minutes later he saw my car coming down the street in the opposite direction, getting ready to pull up at the house. He tried calling Riana again, but still couldn't reach her.

With the guys still in the house, I parked in my driveway on the side of the house. My sisters and I just came from spending the day together. Just as I was about to shut the car off, one of the gunmen shouted upstairs.

"Here she is."

Seeing the gun in his hand, I quickly put the car in reverse and sped off. Mr. B. and the guys came down stairs as quick as they could and jumped in their cars and chased the girls.

Frank's truck would not crank fast enough to get behind us but he got it cranked just in time to follow the guys. The two drivers caught up with us because they were professional getaway drivers. To avoid running stop signs and traffic signals, and getting in a wreck and hurting someone, I jumped on the main expressway. When both of the cars pulled up on opposite sides, ordering me to pull over, Riana noticed the same black SUV Anthony was in at the drug exchange. She knew then why they were being chased, so she told me everything. I broke down in tears, but knew there was no time for arguing or asking questions. Traffic was still kind of heavy at that time, so the guys pulled back but trailed her very closely.

I thought I could shake them, so I attempted a last minute turn to exit off the highway, but it did not work. Both cars were still tight on our trail. The direction in which we were headed was towards an old warehouse district that had been shut down for many years. No traffic was allowed in this area. There was only one road, one way in and one way out. At the end of the road, was the canal.

Pulling up to both sides again to sandwich the car, the drivers rammed her car, sending sparks in the air. I still wouldn't pull over, so one of the gunmen shot out my back tire and the driver hit her car on the right rear, sending the car spinning out of control in a circle, until it finally crashed into a building.

The car hit the building so hard that an explosion occurred under the hood. Smoke from the fire began to spread through the vents. We quickly got out and ran inside the building. The warehouse was an old, two-story building that was used to house imported goods until inspected by Customs. We decided to split up because the chances of getting away would be better than if we would have stuck together.

Mr. B. and his gunman came in shortly after. Each of them separated and searched every corner of the building. I hid on the second floor behind some wooden crates. Riana was just across from me, hiding behind another set of crates. Briana was still on the first floor trying to find somewhere to hide. Out of nowhere, one of the gunmen grabbed her and brought her to the middle of the warehouse where Mr. B. was waiting.

Through a crack between the crates, Riana and I watched Briana being held at gunpoint. Riana couldn't just sit there and watch, so she made a brave attempt to save her. Quietly, creeping down stairs, she snuck up on one of the gunman and put her gun to his head ordering him to drop his gun or she was going to shoot. The man complied with her. Riana then told them to let Briana go and they did. As soon as she walked towards her, one of the gunmen came from behind her with his gun to the back of her head and made her drop her gun. Now, they had them lying face down on the floor demanding me to come out in five seconds or they were going to kill both of them.

Back at my house Frank had called in a favor to his drinking buddies. Two of them were his friends since childhood and gangbanging days. Even though they weren't living the gangster lifestyle anymore, they always promised to have each other's back, no matter how or when it was. Since his friends lived near the warehouses, it didn't take long for them to get there.

Within the five-second count, I came out with my hands in the air. Once I got downstairs, the gunman tied me up next to my sisters. Mr. B. wanted to know the reason his son was murdered. He started asking Riana questions, but she wouldn't answer him. As he walked around me, he took a good look at me and said, *"You look very familiar. Where are you from?"*

"New York."

"I used to run my operation out of New York about 22 years. The police were getting too hot after the Franklin Projects homicide. That was my last job there."

When he said that, a flashback played through my mind and suddenly I remembered the voice and the scar on the left side of his face.

"You bastard. That was my father you killed," I said in a crying voice.

"I knew you looked familiar. You're old Willie's daughter. What is this? DeJavu?

I had your mother and my son had you. It doesn't get any better than this. Too bad your pops couldn't be here to see this."

Before Mr. B. pulled the trigger, Frank and his

friends came up behind them and said, *"Drop your guns. I won't ask anymore."*

Mr. B. and his crew were on one side and Frank and his guys on the other. We were sitting in the middle of the crossfire. Mr. B. shook his head at Frank and told him, *"You shouldn't stick your nose where it doesn't belong. I thought I taught you that."*

"My daughter is my business and now I'm about to teach you a lesson."

Through their short conversation, neither of them lowered their guns. Frank told one of his guys to untie us. He started with Briana and then me. When he got to Riana Mr. B. gave his guys a head nod, meaning take the shot the first chance you get. When he untied Riana, she hurried towards Frank to give him a hug. When he reached to hug her, his gun lowered and one of the gunmen took a shot at him, hitting him in the shoulder. Instantly, gunshots from both sides rang out towards each other. It was like a scene from an old western movie.

We took off running as soon as the first shot was fired. Riana took Frank to a safe spot to check out his wound and tried to find something to keep pressure on the hole so it could temporarily stop bleeding. She found an old blanket and gave him her shirt. After that, she took his gun and went off to find us.

Five out of six of Mr. B's men were shot and killed instantly. The only two left were he and Orvy. He knew he was out numbered, but didn't care. All by himself, Orvy walked up on Frank sitting on the floor. While Frank was pretending to be dying, Orvy kneeled over him, for minutes, taunting him. As soon as he raised his gun to shoot, two shots came from under the blanket hitting him in the chest. Frank always kept a backup on him. This was one of the things Mr. B. taught him.

Crawling from behind one crate to another, Mr. B snuck up behind me. He shoved me to the ground and stood over me with his gun pointed at my head and said, *"You are starting to piss me off. Get on the ground. You killed my son? Now, you are about to join him and your father."*

Before he could get the shot off, three final shots pierced him in the back, killing him instantly. Riana had come to my rescue at the perfect time. She then picked me up off the ground and went over to help her father. Once she heard our voices, Briana came out from hiding. Only one of Frank's friends survived. The police showed up after all the shooting was over. Apparently, the alarm system was still activated after all these years.

On the way to the hospital, Riana asked me to tell her the story of how my father was murdered. I told the both of them everything.

"When I was about 8 years my father was involved in

dealing drugs. One night, I came in the house and three guys had him and our mother tied up. My father couldn't have any more kids because of an accident he had shortly after I was born. Before they shot my dad, one of them raped my mother. Later, she found out that she was pregnant by that man. The man you just killed happens to be your father. Since Anthony was his son, that made him your brother. Mom died shortly after she gave birth to you two, leaving me to be raised by our grandmother and the two of you separated into two families. Now here we are. I'm so glad that we found each other. I love you two so much. Even though we can't run from our past, now we have each other and a chance for a new beginning. I think it's safe to say that we have formed an eternal bond of sisterhood, love, and life that can never be broken."

Discussion Questions

1. Being that the author is a male, why do you think he chose to write a story about women?

2. Based on the description of women in the novel, how well do you think the author knows women? How and why is he able to relate to women so well?

3. As a grandmother, why do you think she decided to give up the twins and keep Samantha?

4. Why do you think Frank put his life on the line for a child that he didn't want to begin with?

5. Do you think adoptive parents have the right to withhold information from their adopted child about its biological family?

6. Despite his upbringing, do you think Anthony's love for Samantha was genuine?

7. If Riana would have known Mr. B was her father, do you think she still would have killed him to save Samantha's life?

8. Do you think all children follow in the footsteps or their parents in some way or another? For example, even though Riana didn't know Mr. B was her father, she lived a life of crime as he did.

9. Is there such a thing as a family curse? If so, what evidence did this family show to make you believe or disbelieve that theory?

10. Some people believe that what is meant to be, will be. Do you think if Briana had never overheard Danielle and Susan talking about her sisters, would they have found each other anyway?

11. If you can be any character in the story, who will you choose and why? By choosing that character, what do you see in them that you can relate to yourself?

12. Did this novel keep your attention from the beginning until the end? By the way the story ended, do you think there will be a sequel?

NOTES

NOTES

NOTES

NOTES

NOTES

NOTES

NOTES

NOTES

NOTES

NOTES

NOTES

Printed in the United States
201164BV00001B/193-297/P

9 781432 718909